STRENGTH

and

ENCOURAGEMENT

Poetry for the Journey of Faith

LAURA GASQUE

ISBN 978-1-63630-166-2 (Paperback)
ISBN 978-1-63630-167-9 (Hardcover)
ISBN 978-1-63630-168-6 (Digital)

Scripture quotations unless noted otherwise are from the *Holy Bible*, New Living Translation ©1996, 2004, 2007 by Tyndale House Foundation. Used by permission of Tyndale House Publishers, Inc., Carol Stream, Illinois 60188. All rights reserved.

Scripture quotations marked NRSV are from the New Revised Standard Version of the Bible, copyright 1989, Division of Christian Education of the National Council of the Churches of Christ in the United States of America. Used by permission. All rights reserved.

Scripture quotations marked NIV are from the HOLY BIBLE, NEW INTERNATIONAL VERSION ®. Copyright ©1973, 1978, 1984 by International Bible Society. Used by permission of Zondervan Publishing House. All rights reserved.

Cover photo by Laura Gasque of bridge at Lake Junaluska, NC

Covenant Books, Inc.
11661 Hwy 707
Murrells Inlet, SC 29576
www.covenantbooks.com

CONTENTS

PREFACE

We all need strength and encouragement for this journey of life, our journey of faith. No matter who we are or what age or stage in which we are presently living, everyone needs some help along the way. This can come from any number of sources available to us. It may be from our spouses, our friends, our children, our extended family, our neighbors, or our coworkers who are there when we feel weak or discouraged. Perhaps reading books by well-known Christians are what gives us a lift. Attending spiritual retreats, listening to sermons, reading scripture, and singing hymns may give us hope. Our prayers and the prayers of others can open doors of healing and grace.

Christian poems can bring strength and encouragement in our faith journey too. After all, many hymns are simply poems put to music. And the book of Psalms is considered poetry. How many times have we received light during the darkness by reading Psalms or by singing the hymns? This is my purpose too. With the poems included in this book, my hope is to bring strength and encouragement to others in their journey of faith through this poetry that is a gift from the Lord.

I didn't begin my educational journey with the burning desire of being a poet. None of my teachers in high school or college ever suggested I become a writer, a poet, or a journalist. When I became a poet was when I started my spiritual journey with my Lord Jesus Christ. After I surrendered my life to Jesus in 1992 was when I discovered this new talent of writing spiritual poems. The beginning line of a new poem would just appear in my thoughts. So I would sit down, listen, and write. I was totally amazed at this gift God had given me! And for many years, I thought about publishing but never did.

For about twenty-seven years, I have been writing these messages from the Lord in poetry form. At certain times like Christmas or Easter, I would share one of these poems with family or friends or church members. Sometimes I would read one very special poem at funerals. But pretty much, most of them have been kept in a safe place at home and on my computer, hidden or buried.

The words *buried* or *hidden* are what I considered for years on end. In the parable of the talents from Matthew 25, the person who is entrusted with one talent "went off and dug a hole in the ground and hid his master's money" (verse 18 NRSV). This servant or slave had not used the gift the master had given. What the master had entrusted with this person had been hidden or buried. Nothing increased. Nothing was invested. Nothing happened to bring the master great joy when he returned. For an extended period, I felt that I had buried this talent, even though I had shared some of these poems at times. Much more could have been done to spread this message of strength and encouragement from Him.

I was afraid of publishing the poetry because I didn't think a book of poems would interest many people. I didn't believe people read poetry books much anymore. And I surely didn't know how to publish. So the fear of failure and being busy with other work for the Lord kept a lot of the poetry hidden for twenty-seven years. But the thought of hiding what the Lord had given me was always in the back of my mind. And I did want to publish at some point in time... eventually. Procrastination is not a good thing.

One night, in February 2018, at a prayer group, one of my friends made a comment, thanking someone else in the group for regularly sending her elderly mother a card. Her mother appreciated so much being remembered. This planted a seed in my spirit that grew immediately. I could do the same thing with my poems. I could send my poems through the mail to older people who were at home or in a facility. They probably had plenty of time on their hands, might be lonely, and may want to receive encouraging Christian mail on a regular basis. I found a group of people who might spend time reading the poems every month! One at a time. Not in a thick book. And I could write some personal note at the same time too. I finally found a way to share what God had so generously given to me! And I didn't have to publish them!

What began as a way to share my poetry with a few church members and friends has expanded into what I consider a new ministry for the Lord in my life. Many people have been added to this ever-growing list of those who regularly receive a Christian poem through the mail. And the blessing for me is that new poems keep coming faster than I can send them out!

After receiving much affirmation from those receiving the poems and encouragement from my supportive husband, Paul, who has already published, I decided to finally do what I believe God wanted me to do all along. I believe His purpose for giving me these poems is to share them with many other believers. This is one way of spreading the good news of Jesus Christ. These poems have helped me immensely in my own faith journey. It is my prayer and hope that you will be strengthened and encouraged in your own walk with the Lord by these poems too.

INTRODUCTION

Life is a journey of many steps. From the moment we are born until the last step we take here on earth, this journey is one we make in the presence of Jesus Christ. He sees and knows each one of us. He walks with us as we continue day by day, season by season, growing and maturing. Some recognize and acknowledge His presence early on and walk hand in hand with Him for the rest of their days. Others do not sense His love and patience in their lives until many years have passed. The day finally comes when they walk out of darkness and enter the light. Then there are the ones who never know His presence and live without hope. In this journey we call life, no matter who we are, we need the strength and encouragement that Jesus and those who follow Him can give us.

This spiritual journey we make with Christ is the daily walk of a lifetime. When we follow Him on the path where He leads, we go up high mountains and down in deep valleys. We experience the joy and gladness and the sorrow and the pain. Some of our journeys seem to pass by too fast and other journeys feel like they will never end. The one constant is that He is with us always and never leaves us. We need His strength and encouragement as we make this marathon journey that leads to eternal life for those who are His disciples.

The poems in this book are meant to bring the readers strength and encouragement in the many journeys in their lifetime. In the spiritual realm, we do not stay at the same place in our walk with Christ. We grow and mature. Jesus leads and guides us and takes us on a multitude of paths that require our faith and trust in Him as our Savior. Sometimes we are excited to go to that place of joy with Him. In other moments, we do not want to even think about the unexpected things that could happen and where the present journey will end. Such is life. That's why we need Jesus. That's why we need strength and encouragement along the way. Then we will never quit or give up or turn away from the One whose ultimate strength is seen in the cross. Be strengthened and encouraged in your journey today.

CHAPTER 1

THE JOURNEY OF NEW BEGINNINGS AND CHANGE

Our journey of new beginnings starts with an ending. Something must be completed and finished before there is a new beginning. We have to give up one stage of life before we enter into the next one. When a child is born, the pregnancy ends. When adulthood begins, we are finished with our teenaged years. When we have completed our education and graduate, we are no longer students. If we get married, we cease to be single. If we have children, we leave behind the childless life and become something we never were—parents. If we have a new job, we leave behind the old one. New beginnings are exciting. We look forward to that day of promise. We make plans and celebrate. We are in the process of changing and becoming new people, taking on different roles and responsibilities. Maybe living out our dream.

These new beginnings create drastic changes in our lives. Even though we are happy about this new thing, we are walking into unchartered territory. We have never been this way before. We have to say goodbye to the old way and hello to the new way. We leave our comfortable position in life and take on the unknown. We leave behind some people and places with which we were familiar to take a path we've not yet traveled. Life calls us away from our ordinary existence to what is beyond the horizon. It's something we cannot see now, and it takes courage and faith to step out into the deep waters. Anxiety and questions may overwhelm us at times. It is all a part of the journey as we live into the person we are becoming.

Our Christian life is like this. When we make a new beginning with Christ, we part with our old ways of doing things. We make a change from worldly to sacred, from self-centered to Christ-centered, and we keep on changing for the rest of our lives. In this journey with Christ, we will forevermore make new beginnings as we are being made into His image. Second Corinthians 5:17 reminds us, "This means that anyone who belongs to Christ has become a new person. The old life is gone; a new life has begun!" It doesn't say "a new life is here all at once today, complete in everything." The wording is, "a new life has begun!" New beginnings for the rest of our lives!

Prayer for the New Year

I praise you for
This beautiful day.
I thank You, Lord,
For showing the way.
O Lord, I'm blessed
That I can pray.
Thank You for giving me
Words to say.

Forgive me, Father,
When I don't see
The person You're trying
To help me be.
The blood that was spilled
Upon the tree
Is the power I need
For victory.

I bring to Your throne
Those who are lost.
I pray one day
They'll know the cost
Of a Savior who died
Upon the cross
So their soul to hell
Cannot be tossed.

I pray for the bereaved,
The sick, the ill,
For medical people
And others who heal,

For the homeless, the poor
Without a meal,
For the angry ones
Who hurt and steal.

I pray for those
Who live with pain.
Enable them all
To rest again.
Please give them hope
That is not in vain
While on earth
In this body
They remain.

I pray for my family
Wherever they are
That Your light would be
A luminous star
To guide them whether
They're near or far,
By foot, by plane,
By subway, by car.

O Father, I say
These prayers to You
Knowing You always
Know what to do.
Give me grace and peace.
Make me new.
To Your will
I'll always be true.

Get Rid Of

"Get rid of," He said,
As I sat down to pray.
Today was not just
Any ordinary day.
This was the end of
The old year, for sure.
A new one was coming.
This was the cure.

I thought to myself
I've gotten rid of some things,
Old papers, old clothes,
What clutter it brings!
I've given away books.
I've thrown away trash.
I've finally lessened
What I call my stash.

Clean closets, clean drawers,
Clean bedrooms and such.
I've removed all this stuff.
So thankful! It's much!
What more does the Lord
Want from me now?
I could clean out those cabinets.
He'll show me how.

But wait. As I picked up
My Bible one day.
Was there something in here
I remembered Him say?

"*Get rid of* these sins.
They're blocking My light.
Don't hide in this darkness
When things could be bright."

What was He showing me?
How could I know?
So many words in here
Could help me to grow.
In my life as a Christian
I've given Him my heart.
But sometimes I need space
To make a new start.

So just like those closets
Filled with old things,
I bring Him myself and
The stuff that still clings
To that place in my heart,
To that place in my head
That keeps my life cluttered.
What was it He said?

"*Get rid of* the way
You live your life
When anger takes hold
And you live in great strife.
Forgive all the people
Who've made you real mad.
Don't speak any words
That are false or are bad.

"Be the holy one
I have called you to be.
Show mercy and kindness.
Have a heart like Me.

Be gentle and patient.
Be peaceful and love.
Get rid of the things
That are not from above.

"*Get rid of* your sin
And My promise to you
Is more space for My grace
And a person who is new."

SPREAD YOUR WINGS

Spread your wings and fly.
You're not a child anymore.
Don't look at the ground.
Look to the sky.
Believe in Him and soar.

Spread your wings and fly.
The Lord is waiting to see.
He's helped you grow.
He's given you wings.
Courageous He wants you to be.

Spread your wings and fly.
Now it's up to you.
Do you want to walk
Or do you want to soar?
What does He want you to do?

Spread your wings and fly.
Sometimes it's a scary thing.
What if I fail
Or can't get very high?
What shame you think that would bring.

Spread your wings and fly.
Trust Him. Have faith. No fear.
No pain. No gain.
Believe in Him.
Let His plan and purpose be clear.

Spread your wings and fly.
For this is why you were born.
He created you
With this in mind.
He's there with you in each storm.

Spread your wings and fly
Even though it's something new.
Let go of your fears.
Get out of the nest.
He'll show you what to do.

Spread your wings and fly.
You're free to rise up and be
The one He's called,
The one He loves,
The one He wants to see.

Spread your wings and fly.
You'll never be the same.
The heights you'll reach
The sights you'll see
You'll bless His holy name.

Spread your wings and fly.
The time is getting near.
It's you this time
And not someone else.
Let go of all you hold dear.

Spread your wings and fly.
There can be no other way
For you to know the joy,
For you to accomplish His plan.
Today could be the day.

Spread your wings and fly.
The best is yet to come.
One day, He'll call,
And you'll fly away
To your eternal home.

Spread your wings and fly.

GO FORWARD NOW

My child, I love you.
Go forward now.
I know why
And I know how.
Depend upon Me
And soon you'll know.
The blessings are many,
The ones I bestow.
Hear me now
And weep a tear.
You can't go back
To doubt and fear.
Your name is written
In the Book of Life.
Live your days
Without this strife.

I've taken you from
A tiny little girl
To a mature woman
Living in the world.
Be who you are
And you will see
What I can do
With one who's free.
Free to love.
Free to pray.
Free from the burden
You've carried
each day.

Go forward now.
Do not look back.
I've called you now.
You're on My track.
Enter this season
Of your life with Me.
I'll bless you with life
Abundantly.
Your faith is shown
By what you do,
By how you act.
I'll get you through.
Leave this valley of tears
And return to Me.
I've called you on high.
By My grace, you will see.

Your days of trial
Are soon to end.
I *am* your Savior.
I *am* your friend.
Look to the future
With peace in your eyes.
The blessings I bestow
Will surely surprise.
My reward will be with you
In the days ahead.
I've seen your obedience
In your heart and your head.

Go forward now.
Be who you are.
Accept this gift.
Be a shining star.
What was taken away
Will be given to you,

Blessed and multiplied,
Not just for a few.
Like the fish and the loaves,
In My hand, you'll see,
I will bless the gift
You've given to Me.
Crowds will be fed.
Many will draw near
When I bless what you give
My voice they will hear.

Leave the past.
Go forward today.
Remember I love you.
Always pray.
These people need Me
And you are the one
To share with them
My only Son.
I've opened this door.
Come on through.
This is your life,
Redeemed and new.

Scripture about New Beginnings and Change

He has given me a new song to sing, a hymn of praise to our God. Many will see what he has done and be amazed. They will put their trust in the Lord.

—Psalm 40:3

But forget all that—it is nothing compared to what I am going to do. For I am about to do something new. See, I have already begun! Do you not see it? I will make a pathway through the wilderness. I will create rivers in the dry wasteland.

—Isaiah 43:18

"But this is the new covenant I will make with the people of Israel on that day," says the Lord. "I will put my instructions deep within them, and I will write them on their hearts. I will be their God, and they will be my people."

—Jeremiah 31:33

After supper, he took another cup of wine and said, "This cup is the new covenant between God and his people—an agreement confirmed with my blood, which is poured out as a sacrifice for you."

—Luke 22:20

That is why he is the one who mediates a new covenant between God and his people, so that all who are called can receive the eternal inheritance God has promised them.

—Hebrews 9:15

For we died and were buried with Christ by baptism. And just as Christ was raised from the dead by the glorious power of the Father, now we may also live new lives.

—Romans 6:4

It doesn't matter if we have been circumcised or not. What counts is whether we have been transformed into a new creation.

—Galatians 6:15

Throw off your old sinful nature and your former way of life, which is corrupted by lust and deception. Instead, let the Spirit renew your thoughts and attitudes. Put on your new nature, created to be like God—truly righteous and holy.

—Ephesians 4:22–24

Put on your new nature and be renewed as you learn to know your Creator and become like him.

—Colossians 3:10

By his death, Jesus opened a new and life-giving way through the curtain into the Most Holy Place.

—Hebrews 10:20

CHAPTER 2

THE JOURNEY OF CONFESSION AND REPENTANCE

What Do I Look At?
A Tree with Many Years
Waters of Life
Why Do I Complain?
Scripture about Confession and Repentance

The journey of confession and repentance requires a truthful and honest examination of ourselves considering who our Holy Father has called us to be. In today's world, many do not have the time or the desire to attempt to do such a thing. In looking closely at our sins against God and others, we must throw away our pride and admit that we are wrong and guilty. It is necessary that we reconsider the things we have said or done. Or perhaps our greatest confession is that we have not spoken or acted. Silence and apathy or uncaring hearts. Confession is the first step in returning to the Lord, in having a closer relationship with Him. Instead of hiding our sin, we bring it out into the open and talk to God. First John 1:9 says, "But if we confess our sins to him, he is faithful and just to forgive us our sins and to cleanse us from all wickedness." In this journey of confession, we need a lot of cleansing.

Repentance goes along with confession. If we confess with our mouth that we have sinned against God and others, then we are aware of the barriers we have erected that separate us. But it is necessary that we repent of this sin and change direction and turn back toward our Father God. We must make changes and adjustments in our way of acting, speaking, and thinking. Repentance makes our journey a different one. Instead of traveling south, we take the exit ramp and change directions and travel north. That's how drastic repentance should be. We turn back to God.

Psalm 51 is a prayer for cleansing and pardon or forgiveness. We are seeking forgiveness from our Holy Father when we sincerely confess and repent of our sins. Psalm 51:1–2, 10–11, 17 (NRSV) says, "Have mercy on me, O God, according to your steadfast love; according to your abundant mercy blot out my transgressions. Wash me thoroughly from my iniquity, and cleanse me from my sin. Create in me a clean heart, O God, and put a new and right spirit within me. Do not cast me away from your presence, and do not take your holy spirit from me. The sacrifice acceptable to God is a broken spirit; a broken and contrite heart, O God, you will not despise."

Our hearts need to be broken and contrite because of our sins and rebellion against God. We are guilty, but the blood of Jesus cleanses us of all our sins! This journey of confession and repentance leads to forgiveness.

WHAT DO I LOOK AT?

What do I look at?
The body or the heart?
The inner and the outer
Is all just a part
Of the one who is made
In the image of God
Who is loved by Him
In this journey we trod.

The inside of me
Is what you can't see
Unless you look deep
To find if I'm free
Of the ways of the world
That take hold of the soul.
Can you tell if I'm loved?
If I'm lonely or cold?

Can you see through my eyes
To the places I've been?
Is there hurt and abuse
That's been all held within?
When you look at my body,
It's fading. That's true.
What used to be young
Is no longer new.

Does the outside of me
Matter in His eyes?
It's the inner that receives
His glorious prize,
The life that He lived
So I wouldn't die.
I'm beautiful to Him.
I don't need to cry.

You can't see the inner
I try hard to hide.
A smile on my face
But weeping inside.
Although I may not be
Pretty to see
I need kindness and caring.
Someone who loves me.

Every person who lives
In this big world today
Has these feelings sometimes
Whatever they say.
The inner and outer
May not be at peace,
In prison, still lonely
Seeking release.

So love every person
That you see today.
Help them. Don't hurt them
As we travel the way.
Be kind and compassionate
And look in their heart.
Don't dwell on the outside.
Don't set them apart.

The ones we are looking at
Could be us someday.
We need to hold hands
So together we can pray.
Uplift your brother
And sister today
As we travel
   the long
      narrow way.

A Tree with Many Years

The red tip tree
In my backyard
Looks different
This morning to me.
No green leaves.
No flowers and bees.
It's dark and gray.
Not producing today.
A tree that's seen
Brighter days.

But it's still there
Branches and limbs
Hardened or
Filled with air,
But growing and green
Nowhere.
There's a purpose
It has for me.
What kind of life
Remains for this tree?
What happened to make it
Become like this?
Years in the weather?
Is something amiss?
It had water and sun,
Plenty at times.
But the sun
Cannot always shine.

Maybe pests or bugs
Or soil washed away
Could have caused it
To be this way.

It's spring, not winter.
Leaves could be there.
But this tree
Is obviously bare.
Is there a reason
For *this* season
In the air?

But wait…
Is that a little bird
I see
Making a nest
In this weathered-down tree?
A nest with babies
And a family?
And here's another
Who could be a mother
Finding shelter in this tree!
I see a red bird,
A brown and a blue!
I hear them singing!
This is true!
I see this tree
Giving shelter and shade,
A refuge from enemies.
A prayer being prayed.

A tree with many years
Branches of gray
Spoke to me today.
It's beautiful in every way.

Sturdy and strong
As it's been all along
Enduring through cold winter days.
How much it has to praise!
Its roots keep it strong
And living for long,
Longer than I could see.

This tree will one day
Be me.

WATERS OF LIFE

Our life is like the waters,
Soft and gentle they sometimes flow.
We're peaceful, and we're happy
No worries and no woe.
But then without a warning,
There's a change upon the sea.
The wave that I was floating on
Comes crashing down on me.
No longer am I up above
But in the dark and deep.
No longer bright and sunny,
But shadows begin to creep.
I'm lost and all alone.
Underneath it, I can't see.
It consumes and surrounds me.
It pulls and drags and covers me.

Just when I think I've had it,
I'm drowning in the roar.
I've spit and swallowed gallons.
Then I'm washed upon the shore.
I take a breath and breathe the air,
The sand upon my face.
I'm on solid ground again
In a safe and peaceful place.
I look back upon the ocean.
It's calm and clear once more.
What happened to me then?
What caused that mighty roar?

Others were around me
But they didn't notice me.
They didn't know what happened

Underneath the mighty sea.
I wonder if I screamed.
I wonder if I yelled.
Did I just succumb to this,
This fury from out of hell?
In quietness and solitude
I walked upon the shore.
I looked back at the ocean
To think of it once more:
I knew that I was drowning.
In the throes of death, I'd been.
I don't understand what happened.
I don't want to go again.

As I close my eyes and speak to God,
I pray to Him who knows.
I ask my tender Father
Who released me from my foes.
He said, "Dear child, I tried to speak,
But you wouldn't hear My voice.
You were safe for a while,
But then you made a choice.
You went out into the deep.
You went way above your head.
You didn't watch the shore.
You didn't listen to what I'd said.
You floated into waters
Too treacherous for you.
You thought you wouldn't drown.
Your pride consumed you too.
Just sit upon the shore
And reflect on who I *am*.
I'm mighty, and I'm powerful.
I'm holy, and I'm grand.

"Nothing is impossible
But you need to trust in Me.
Give it up and let it go
And float once more upon the sea.
Let Me take you out and bring you in.
The tide is in My hand.
Let Me give you peace and rest.
Let My word be your command.
Let Me do it every time.
Your strength alone just will not do.
I have all the power and wisdom.
What you have won't get you through.
Don't look beyond the place
Where I have you on the sea.
Don't try to go too deep.
It's dangerous. You'll see.
Be happy where you are.
Be content and feel My love.
Don't be pulled down underneath
But be embraced by what's above."

As I opened up my eyes
And looked back upon the sea,
I was sitting on the shore.
The water slowly came to me.
This time, I was at peace.
This time, I felt His hand.
His voice was soft and gentle:
"Be still and know I *am*."

WHY DO I COMPLAIN?

Why do I complain, Lord?
You hear the words I say.
I need to be about Your work.
I really ought to pray.
It makes me sad and angry
When others will not do
The things You have commanded
If they truly do love You.

I try to do my part
And use the gifts You give.
I want Your light to shine
Each moment that I live.
But often I am silent
Or will not volunteer.
When I say, "No, not me,"
I'm sure my words You hear.

Some people serve a lot.
They're in the world each day.
They're helping other people,
Showing them the way,
The way to peace and love,
The hope to persevere,
The closeness of our Lord,
Knowing He's always near.

So many lonely ones
Are living in the dark.
Why don't I go and visit
And bring a little spark
Of love and light from You
To brighten up an hour,
With cheer and with laughter
With the Spirit and Your power?

There's so much left to do
If my eyes could only see.
How would Jesus act?
How am I to be?
A smile, a helping hand,
A gentle encouraging word,
Precious moments with them,
Knowing their voice is heard.

I can't do it all, Lord,
But I can do my part.
When I pray and read
That's a way to start.
Forgive me when I fuss
And want to place the blame.
I'm sorry for the words I say.
I guess it brings You shame.

So help me, Lord, right now
To remember how You died.
You gave us all You had.
The tears You must have cried
When people would not listen:
"Repent and follow me."
They chose another life,
And You hung upon that tree.

You gave us everything.
Shouldn't I do the same?
It's not about what they do.
I've heard You call my name.
So here I am. Please send me
Into the world today.
I won't complain or grumble.
I'll follow You all the way.

Scripture about Confession and Repentance

Finally, I confessed all my sins to you and stopped trying to hide my guilt. I said to myself, "I will confess my rebellion to the Lord." And you forgave me! All my guilt is gone.

—Psalm 32:5

The high and lofty one who lives in eternity, the Holy One, says this: I live in the high and holy place with those whose spirits are contrite and humble. I restore the crushed spirit of the humble and revive the courage of those with repentant hearts.

—Isaiah 57:15

From then on Jesus began to preach, "Repent of your sins and turn to God, for the Kingdom of Heaven is near."

—Matthew 4:17

But if we confess our sins to him, he is faithful and just to forgive us our sins and to cleanse us from all wickedness. If we claim we have not sinned, we are calling God a liar and showing that his word has no place in our hearts.

—1 John 1:9–10

People who conceal their sins will not prosper, but if they confess and turn from them, they will receive mercy.

—Proverbs 28:13

Now repent of your sins and turn to God, so that your sins may be wiped away.

—Acts 3:19

I preached…that all must repent of their sins and turn to God—and prove they have changed by the good things they do.

—Acts 26:20

In the same way, there is joy in the presence of God's angels when even one sinner repents.

—Luke 15:10

Don't you see how wonderfully kind, tolerant, and patient God is with you? Does this mean nothing to you? Can't you see that his kindness is intended to turn you from your sin?

—Romans 2:4

But I have this complaint against you. You don't love me or each other as you did at first! Look how far you have fallen! Turn back to me, and do the works you did at first. If you don't repent, I will come and remove your lampstand from its place among the churches.

—Revelation 2:4–5

For the kind of sorrow God wants us to experience leads us away from sin and results in salvation. There is no regret for that kind of sorrow. But worldly sorrow, which lacks repentance, results in spiritual death.

—2 Corinthians 7:10

CHAPTER 3

THE JOURNEY OF FORGIVENESS

Forgiven
When Jesus Forgives Us
Weeping Hearts
God's Grace
Scripture about Forgiveness

What do we know about forgiveness? That it's very hard to do. But because Jesus has forgiven us, we are required to forgive others. If we could count or remember all the times we have been forgiven by God's grace and mercy, we might be more inclined to forgive those who have hurt us. After all, we don't want to be condemned or judged. We seek forgiveness for ourselves, not what we really deserve when we have sinned and should suffer consequences.

Forgiving goes against the grain of what we really feel like doing. We may want the one who destroyed us to suffer just like we have. Our wish might be that they experience pain to the same degree that we have. Perhaps revenge and retaliation are our battle cries. But this is not the way Jesus lived nor the way He has called us to live.

In forgiving, we are placing the person who may have deliberately caused us deep wounds and terrible heartaches into God's hands to deal with as He pleases. Our presumed right to punish and condemn has been forfeited forever and given to the One who knows and sees everything. Only God is aware of all that happened. Only the Lord knows the inner depths of our souls. Only He knows the whole truth.

With forgiveness comes a freedom that can eventually restore our joy for living the abundant life. Once again, a burden can be taken off our heart and mind, and "God's peace, which is far more wonderful than the mind can understand" (Philippians 4:7), can replace it. It may not happen overnight. It could be a long journey toward healing, but if we can envision that person in the hands of God, it may be sooner than we originally thought. Can you imagine a better place for anyone to be?

FORGIVEN

"Forgiven," He said
As I lifted my head.

I came to the Lord
With my guilt and my shame.
I could bear it no more.
It wouldn't happen again.
A burden it had placed
On my life and my soul.
With these feelings inside,
I could never be whole.

I was angry. I was mad.
They had hurt me. They were bad.
Like a knife, they had cut me.
Like a whip, they had struck me
With their words,
With their fears,
With their lies,
With their jeers.
They had taken my peace.
I was in prison with no release.

What could I do but fight them back?
I wouldn't let them. I wouldn't crack.
I defended myself. I was right.
I would show them a real good fight.
But suddenly the Lord appeared to me.
"This isn't the way. Can't you see?
I gave My life. I shed My blood.
I didn't fight but gave them love.
They didn't know. Their eyes were blind.
Their way was wrong. They didn't find

The peace that comes from deep within
When you forget your hate and lay down your sin.

"Come here, sister. See My side.
From this wound, you can abide.
Feel the hole in My hand.
My blood flowed to heal this land.
I forgave them. So can you.
With My Spirit live anew.
With My heart and with My soul
Forgive them now, and you'll be whole."

I forgave them, and now I'm free.
No longer bound. Now I can see.
My anger left. My rage is gone.
No longer bitter or alone.
Jesus showed me how to win.
"Forgive them all for every sin.
Love them more every day.
Lift their name each time you pray,
And you'll be blessed with good things too.
Forgive them all because I forgave you."

WHEN JESUS FORGIVES US

When Jesus forgives us,
Our eyes can see
This mercy doesn't come
From you or me.
It comes from our Father
In the heavenly space.
It comes from our Savior
For the human race.
We don't deserve it.
We're not real strong.
We turn our backs
And do what's wrong.
We think of self.
We rage and sin.
We cover it up
And do it again.

When will we ever
Learn to be
Loving and trusting
And obedient to thee?
When we forget our wants
And leave our pleasures
When we can give it all up
For Your heavenly treasures
When we can touch Your hand
And can accept Your grace
When we fall on our knees
In the holy place
When we let it go
And give it to Him,
Then we can put it to death
And learn to live again.

Weeping Hearts

O Lord, You know
Our weeping hearts
And many the reasons
We cry.
The things that people
Say and do,
The blessings that
Pass us by.

Your weeping heart
Must break apart
When others treat us
This way.
You see the sinful things
They do
And hear each word
They say.

Why must our lives
Be like this, Lord?
We seek Your love
Each day.
The noise and hatred,
Greed and lies
Surround us.
So we pray.

You called us out
Of darkness
And into the light
We came.

I wonder if
Each one of us
Used to play
This game.

We all are sinners
Saved by grace.
The worldly life
We knew.
Until one day,
Forgiveness came,
And now we are
Brand-new.

We still say words
That are not kind
And do things we
Shouldn't do.
O Lord, please help us
When we stray
To obediently follow
You.

God's Grace

Forgiveness comes out of God's grace,
Not for one but for all,
Everywhere, every place.
Redemption is for the sin that we bear
When we fight, when we cheat,
When we just don't care.
Pardon is what we need when we sin
Against God, against self,
Against women or men.
How can we have this
Forgiveness? It's free!
Jesus bled on the cross
To forgive you and me.

Our sin was laid upon His head.
Our sin, how we should cry.
The times we turned away from God,
The times we would not try.
Our sin was nailed into his feet.
Our sin. We should agree.
The things we couldn't give to Him,
The times we wouldn't believe.
Our sin, it pierced His holy side.
Our sin. We bend our knee.
We chose the wrong for far too long.
It's our reality.

His blood, it flowed upon that day.
Not some but all, it fell
To save these sinful souls of ours
From an eternity in hell.

He forgave! He forgave!
He forgave all who see!
Now
I forgive you,
And you forgive me.
Forgiveness comes out of God's grace.
His grace He freely gives
If we forgive each other's sins,
Then we can begin to live.

SCRIPTURE ABOUT FORGIVENESS

And forgive us our sins, as we have forgiven those who sin against us. If you forgive those who sin against you, your heavenly Father will forgive you. But if you refuse to forgive others, your Father will not forgive your sins.

—Matthew 6:12, 14–15

Do not judge others, and you will not be judged. Do not condemn others, or it will all come back against you. Forgive others, and you will be forgiven.

—Luke 6:37

Jesus said, "Father, forgive them, for they don't know what they are doing."

—Luke 23:34

Then Peter came to him and asked, "Lord, how often should I forgive someone who sins against me? Seven times?" "No, not seven times," Jesus replied, "but seventy times seven!"

—Matthew 18:21

But when you are praying, first forgive anyone you are holding a grudge against, so that your Father in heaven will forgive your sins too.

—Mark 11:25

Make allowance for each other's faults and forgive anyone who offends you. Remember, the Lord forgave you, so you must forgive others.

—Colossians 3:13

Instead, be kind to one another, tenderhearted, forgiving one another, just as God through Christ has forgiven you.

—Ephesians 4:32

He forgives all my sins and heals all my diseases.

—Psalm 103:3

And he took a cup of wine and gave thanks to God for it. He gave it to them and said, "Each of you drink from it, for this is my blood, which confirms the covenant between God and his people. It is poured out as a sacrifice to forgive the sins of many."

—Matthew 26:27–28

CHAPTER 4

THE JOURNEY OF EASTER

Easter Blessings Can Happen
The Holy Wonder of Easter
It's Easter, Our Resurrection Day
Easter Is a Hallelujah
Scripture about Easter

The journey of Easter reveals a Jesus no one ever knew. His disciples, His mother, His followers, the women, the people in the crowd, and everyone who was a witness thought He was dead and gone. On Easter Day, He appeared to the women at the tomb, the disciples behind locked doors, and the men on their way to Emmaus. He talked with them and showed them His hands and side. He walked with them and broke bread. No one expected Him to come back from the grave, but He was alive again! Resurrected by the power of God! Easter Day begins with the glorious event that no one could even imagine. It changed everything!

Easter proves to us that God always has the last word. Death does not. Our foes do not. Whatever or whoever would destroy the body do not. Sin does not. Easter shows us God's power over all these things. Since God raised Jesus up from death, He will raise us up too. Those who believe in Jesus as the Son of God and live their life for Him will be resurrected one day also.

On Easter Day, the impossible happened, and God's plan and purpose were revealed. An eternal change had taken place. No one had ever died and been resurrected, but Jesus was! The creation of a new way was in the making. A new life for those who believed in Jesus would begin. The law was replaced by grace and mercy through faith in Christ. The curtain was torn, and now we could approach our Holy Father with boldness and confidence, speaking directly with Him because of the sacrifice of Jesus. Easter was the first day of the new way.

This journey of Easter brings light to our darkness. It gives us peace during despair. Our weeping turns to joy. We have hope beyond what we can see with our eyes or touch with our hands. We have the assurance of a holy place in heaven after this earthly life is over. Because we know this world in which we live is not all that exists, we can look forward to the world to come. Resurrection awaits us when we will be taken to that heavenly place that we have never seen, and we will live with our Father forever. Easter is the reason of our hope for today and all our tomorrows.

EASTER BLESSINGS CAN HAPPEN

Easter blessings can happen
Sometime each hour, each day
The unresponsive people
Can turn away from gray
Their sight can be restored
And colors fill their lives
The young and the old alike
Some husbands and some wives

Easter blessings can happen
When we've had all we can take
We're at the end of trying
We feel we're going to break
Somehow someone prays for us
Something changes deep within
We know the Lord is with us
From this day until the end

Easter blessings can happen
When sadness and grief set in
We've lost so many loved ones
And the future seems real dim
We read the Holy Word
And are patient with God's time
We remember all His promises
And know He's by our side.

Easter blessings can happen
Because of our precious Lord.
He was nailed to the cross
And His side was pierced with sword.
They all thought He was dead
No more of Him to be.
But Jesus appeared beyond the grave
For all the world to see.

Easter blessings can happen
Any time on any day
When we're raised from the death of life
Our heart has seen His way.
We leave behind the darkness
And soar into the sky.
Resurrection happens many times
And not just when we die.

THE HOLY WONDER OF EASTER

The holy wonder of Easter
Is seen throughout the land.
What was lifeless in the winter
Comes alive through His plan.
The ground is suddenly different.
The azaleas and tulips bloom.
All creation is breathing once more
And growth is coming soon.

The holy wonder of Easter
Is the resurrection of our Lord.
He told them it would happen.
They didn't believe His word.
He came up out of the grave
And spoke to all who would hear.
He gave them peace and hope
And helped them to draw near.

The holy wonder of Easter
Is a beautiful sacred day.
Because of our Lord Jesus
We all can have a new way.
The darkness has disappeared.
The eternal light has come.
Resurrection power is ours
Leaving out no one.

The holy wonder of Easter
Is now the people can know
About our heavenly home
To which one day, we can go.

We're sure that life on earth
Will certainly one day cease.
Then Jesus will come back
Taking us to the place of peace.

The holy wonder of Easter
Creates disciples who believe.
The victory is ours to claim
Our sins and fears relieve
The empty tomb was there
On the first dark Easter morn.
He's alive, not dead! He lives today!
Raise the triumphant horn!

It's Easter
Our Resurrection Day

Joyful music in the air
Little children everywhere
Yellows, blues, pinks, and greens
Colorful sights all to be seen

Sunrise service at break of day
Hearing the message and piano play
Pausing for silence, we stop and pray
It's Easter, our resurrection day

Lilies blooming, beautiful and white
Churches decorated, holy and bright
Families gather in this sacred hour
For Jesus, raised with God's power

Eternally grateful for what He's done
Obedient, perfect, the beloved Son
Forever He loves us, the victory won
Inviting all people to come

EASTER IS A HALLELUJAH

Easter is a hallelujah
We remember Jesus raised
The grave couldn't contain Him
All glory, honor, and praise!
We shout with happy voices
The holy music we know
We have a new beginning
We're blessed on earth below.

Easter is our life of hope
Eternal death is gone
Abundant mercy and power
And healing which will come
Our days are filled with promises
Because sometime soon, we'll be
In the presence of our Lord and God
The land of perfect peace

Easter's about creation
In nature, God shows His plan.
Reviving, renewing, restoring
The artwork of His hand.
It's a time of transformation
A time for eyes to see
The changing of the landscape
New life in you and me

A change that's unexpected
We pause with unbelief
Can this be true? We wonder
Such joy after all the grief
A miracle we couldn't imagine
Thoughts racing through our head

Did we hear His voice speaking?
We thought that He was dead.

Easter is a hallelujah
Each morn we open eyes
We walk in faith with Christ
Enduring for the prize
Easter is our reason
To continually praise His name
He's changing us and others
We're raised up and not the same.

Scripture about Easter

The women ran quickly from the tomb. They were very frightened but also filled with great joy, and they rushed to give the disciples the angel's message. And as they went Jesus met them and greeted them. And they ran to him, grasped his feet, and worshipped him. Then Jesus said to them, "Don't be afraid! Go tell my brothers to leave for Galilee, and they will see me there."

—Matthew 28:8–10

After Jesus rose from the dead early on Sunday morning, the first person who saw him was Mary Magdalene, the woman from whom he had cast out seven demons…Afterward he appeared in a different form to two of his followers who were walking from Jerusalem into the country. Still later he appeared to the eleven disciples as they were eating together.

—Mark 16:9, 12, 13

That same day, two of Jesus' followers were walking to the village of Emmaus, seven miles from Jerusalem. As they walked along they were talking about everything that had happened. As they talked and discussed these things, Jesus himself suddenly came and began walking with them. But God kept them from recognizing him.

—Luke 24:13–16

That Sunday evening the disciples were meeting behind locked doors because they were afraid of the Jewish leaders. Suddenly, Jesus was standing there among them! "Peace be with you," he said. As he spoke, he showed them the wounds in his hands and his side. They were filled with joy when they saw the Lord!

—John 20:19–20

Eight days later the disciples were together again, and this time Thomas was with them. The doors were locked; but suddenly, as before, Jesus was standing among them. "Peace be with you," he said. Then he said to Thomas, "Put your finger here, and look at my hands. Put your hand into the wound in my side. Don't be faithless any longer. Believe!" "My Lord and my God!" Thomas exclaimed.

—John 20:26–28

Later, Jesus appeared again to the disciples beside the Sea of Galilee… "Now come and have some breakfast!" Jesus said. None of the disciples dared to ask him, "Who are you?" They knew it was the Lord. Then Jesus served them the bread and the fish. This was the third time Jesus had appeared to his disciples since he had been raised from the dead.

—John 21:1a, 12–14

Then the eleven disciples left for Galilee, going to the mountain where Jesus had told them. When they saw him, they worshipped him-but some of them doubted. Jesus came and told his disciples, "I have been given all authority in heaven and on earth. Therefore, go and make disciples of all nations, baptizing them in the name of the Father and the Son and the Holy Spirit. Teach these new disciples to obey all the commands I have given you. And be sure of this: I am with you always, even to the end of the age."

—Matthew 28:16–20

During the forty days after his crucifixion, he appeared to the apostles from time to time, and he proved to them in many ways that he was actually alive. And he talked to them about the Kingdom of God.

—Acts 1:3

CHAPTER 5

THE JOURNEY OF PRAYER

O Lord, Please Help Me
Prayer Is Like My Candle
Where Does a Prayer End?
What Is Your Prayer for Me?
The Holy Way
Scripture about Prayer

The journey of prayer takes up deep into the loving heart of God. It is His great desire that we talk with Him and share our joys and fears with Him. As we reveal our deep, intimate thoughts, confess our daily sins, and ask for help for ourselves and others, we find our Father listens intently with an ear that hears much more than what we say. He wants to hear our voice, no matter what our words may be. He wants us to share our lives with Him because He is the one who created us. Our Father loves us so much more than anyone else ever could or would. Since He loves us enough to send His Son to take our place on the cross, doesn't He love us enough to hear our prayers with a Father's heart and answer when we pray? This journey of prayer leads us to Him.

Praying is a sacred act that brings us in touch with the Lord God Almighty. When we honestly consider who it is that we are talking with, the God of creation who knows all and sees all, the One who spoke life into being for everyone and everything that exists, we should tremble before Him. His power is far greater than our wildest imagination, a force beyond our ability to understand. This privilege to converse with the Holy One, the One who lives in eternity, whose radiance and glory no one has ever seen, is a gift. It is an invitation to be in the holy place with Him. In this journey of prayer, we enter holiness.

Prayer is a mysterious thing. We know our prayers are going to be answered but not when or how. Sometimes we get a quick response, and other times, we pray for years with no change that we can observe with our earthly eyes. But that's how God works. In His time, in His way, in His will, and in His great plan for the redemption of the world in many instances and in an invisible manner. He always hears and answers our prayers, but we may not recognize the response He gives to the sincere prayer of our heart. His answer may be greater than anything we could ever ask! In this spiritual journey of prayer, we are thankful that He hears and answers every prayer.

Isaiah 55:8–9 reveals to us some things about our prayers and the answers we receive. "My thoughts are nothing like your thoughts," says the Lord. "And my ways are far beyond anything you could imagine. For just as the heavens are higher than the earth, so my ways are higher than your ways and my thoughts higher than your thoughts." This understanding of the Father to whom we pray reveals much. When we pray, we pray in faith trusting in Him. In this journey of prayer, our hope is in Him, His love, and His faithfulness. "For now we see in a mirror, dimly, but then we will see face to face" (1 Corinthians 13:12a NRSV). We trust in Him because our eyes cannot yet see.

O Lord, Please Help Me

O Lord, please help me.
This is what I said.
Keep Your holy words
In my heart and in my head.
There are other words
That daily I hear too,
Words that try to lead me
Away from only You.
Words that are worldly
From many who see
A different kind of life
Without eternity.
Words from the hopeless
Who listen to the lies.
They're lost in the maze
And survival is their prize.

The Lord sends me to these
People in despair,
Calling me from comfort
To help and serve and care.
You always say to love them
But I don't listen to their pain.
I sacrifice for few
Closing the door again.
I can see their struggle
I hear the words they use
I don't try to comfort them
They're desperate for the truth.

Fill me with Your words.
Give me all Your grace.
Send me to the world

To make a better place.
How can people know
The words of our Lord
If I keep them all inside
Not sharing what I've heard?

The evil one who lives
In our world today
Hopes that I am silent
Not teaching what You say.
Some people may not read the Word
Or live a life of peace.
They may not know You, Lord.
No hope of sweet release.

O Lord, please help me
Share the words I hear,
Holy words You give me,
Special words so dear.
They have the power to save.
They show the way to live.
They help me in my fear.
They tell me how to give.
Jesus is the Word,
The truth, the life, the way.
Help me, Jesus, spread the Word
Each and every day.

Prayer Is Like My Candle

Prayer is like the candle
I lit upon this day.
The fragrance I could smell.
The flame would light the way.
But there were things I could not see
When I began my words.
Something was invisible and
A response I never heard.

So suddenly I saw it.
I couldn't believe my eyes!
The power going into the air,
Floating up into the skies.
I tried to look more closely
But found I could not see
Unless I moved my eyes
Away and let it be.

Somewhere beside the candle
I saw this beautiful sight.
A pattern on the table
Illumined by the light.
The sun was shining brightly
Coming through the window near
Making something visible
Making it very clear.

The candle produced a power
I didn't usually see.
And when I blew it out
The smoke helped me believe.
I saw the words I prayed
Don't stay here on the earth.

I saw their force and goodness
And sensed their holy worth.

God sees and hears
The words we say.
He knows our heart
And makes a way
Today, tomorrow
And every day
When we come close
And pray.

Power goes out
We cannot see.
When our eyes fail
We let it be.
Knowing He hears
Is what we need.
The flame still burns.
We can believe.

When we are finished
With our prayer
The scent still lingers
In the air.
It floats above.
We cannot see.
His power
Is loosed and free.

What Is Your Prayer for Me?

O God, what is
Your prayer for me?
To be holy
To be kind
To be gentle
To be good
To show peace
And patience
To be tender
As You would
To be pure
And caring
A servant
Who is daring
Risking all
For the One
Lord Jesus
Your Son
Who gave
Everything
For me.

To be one
With the Lord
To be united
With Him
To assist others
As many
As I can
To be humble
To be meek
Not boasting
But weak

To be thankful
In all things
For the joy
That He brings
Giving God
Everything
I have.

WHERE DOES A PRAYER END?

Where does a prayer end?
Up there.
Somewhere.
Or still lingering around
In the air.
Is there a finality
To a prayer?

We speak these words
Lifted up to Him.
We say them once
And then again.
There is an answer
But we don't know when.
Is eternity where my prayer
Will end?

God knows things
That we don't know.
He is the author
And tells us so
Of our life in heaven
And this one below.
The answer to a prayer
May be slow.

He knows our thoughts
Before we pray.
He speaks to us
Somehow every day
Even if we're busy

And at times a delay.
But His message
Will come some way.

We wait on the Lord
And wonder when.
We've prayed for so long.
How long has it been?
We think back to the time,
How did it begin?
For healing, for hope,
For recognition of sin?

God answers our prayers
As He chooses to.
Some now, some later.
All, not just a few.
The end of a prayer
Will make us feel new.
We are hopeful and peaceful,
Accepting His truth.

But God keeps on showing us
Who we are.
Our prayers are everlasting
They are never too far.
He hears all our words
Sees them like a star
They're eternal in nature
None will ever depart.
A prayer stays deep down
In His heart.

THE HOLY WAY

O Lord, I failed
To pray today.
I didn't ask
For the holy way.
I've made decisions
Not seeking Your will.
Forgive me, God.
I have to be still.

I know I need
To see Your view
Of how I think
And what I do.
I hope my deeds
Bring You glory.
Did I ask for help
In this, Your story?

This life I live
Is written down
In the palms of Your hands.
I'm sure it's bound
In the many pages
Of Your holy book.
I guess I ought
To take a look.

Your story for me
Is loving justice and truth.
It's praying a lot
And pleasing You.
Loving widows and orphans

Living by faith
Showing mercy
Having to wait
Your story is about
The narrow road.
The way is straight
And heavy the load
Giving You our burdens
As we carry some too
Caring for others
Just like You do.

O Lord, I just can't
Decide this thing.
I've pleaded and pondered
Trying to bring
My thoughts in line
With what is holy.
This is my life
But it's really Your story.

I have no answer.
I'll pray again.
You'll show me how.
You'll tell me when.
Lead me and guide me.
I'll trust You, and then
I'll read Your Word
On which I depend.

I see more clearly.
I hear Your voice.
You're with me now.
I have a choice
To follow my Jesus
And carry my cross
Considering the gain
And choosing the loss
Of His life for mine
So I can live.
Your answer is that
I will give.

Scripture about Prayer

The Lord has heard my plea: the Lord will answer my prayer.
—Psalm 6:9

But he delights in the prayers of the upright.
—Proverbs 15:8b

Pray then in this way: Our Father in heaven, hallowed be your name. Your kingdom come. Your will be done, on earth as it is in heaven.
—Matthew 6:9–10 (NRSV)

But if you remain in me and my words remain in you, you may ask for anything you want and it will be granted.
—John 15:7

I appointed you to go and produce lasting fruit, so that the Father will give you whatever you ask for, using my name.
—John 15:16b

Pray in the Spirit at all times and on every occasion. Stay alert and be persistent in your prayers for all believers everywhere.
—Ephesians 6:18

I also tell you this: If two of you agree here on earth concerning anything you ask, my Father in heaven will do it for you. For where two or three gather together as my followers, I am there among them.
—Matthew 18:19–20

Listen to my voice in the morning, Lord. Each morning I bring my requests to you and wait expectantly.
—Psalm 5:3

So let us come boldly to the throne of our gracious God. There we will receive his mercy, and we will find grace to help us when we need it the most.

—Hebrews 4:16

After sending them home, he went up into the hills by himself to pray. Night fell while he was there alone.

—Matthew 14:23

Are any of you suffering hardships? You should pray. Are any of you happy? You should sing praises. Are any of you sick? You should call for the elders of the church to come and pray over you, anointing you with oil in the name of the Lord. Such a prayer offered in faith will heal the sick, and the Lord will make you well. And if you have committed any sins, you will be forgiven.

—James 5:13–15

The earnest prayer of a righteous person has great power and produces wonderful results.

—James 5:16b

Then Jesus went with them to the olive grove called Gethsemane, and he said, "Sit here while I go over there to pray." He went on a little farther and bowed with his face to the ground, praying, "My Father! If it is possible, let this cup of suffering be taken from me. Yet I want your will to be done, not mine."

—Matthew 26:36, 39

CHAPTER 6

THE JOURNEY OF SERVANTHOOD AND CALL

The Candle
It Was God
Has the Lord Spoken Lately?
Be Faithful, My Child
The Camouflaged Ones
The Gift That You Have
Dreams
Scripture about Servanthood and Call

The journey of servanthood is a necessary part of our Christian life. If we have died to self and live for Christ, then we are required to follow the path Jesus walked. We imitate Christ and have the mind of Christ. We choose the sacred lifestyle of service, not the worldly one of honor, prestige, and power. Jesus said, "But among you it will be different. Whoever wants to become a leader among you must be your servant, for even the Son of Man came not to be served but to serve others and to give his life as a ransom for many" (Matthew 20:26, 28).

Our service to God through our service to others means we are sacrificial and humble. Being a servant means being last, not first. It means going places and doing things that others would not even consider. Sometimes servanthood requires us to be with those who are like us, but other times, we are called to be with people who are very different from us. Serving others often takes up a lot of our time. It can be a difficult work that takes much energy, endless patience, and strong endurance. In some circumstances, we are stretched far beyond what we think we can do. Sometimes our service is greatly appreciated but not all the time. In many situations, only God knows how we are serving others because we do not brag or boast.

All Christians have gifts and abilities given to them by the Holy Spirit that empower and enable them to be the servants who are the hands and feet of Christ in the world. And it takes all that we have and all that we are to truly serve God through serving others. It takes our hearts full of love, our eyes that can see the hurt, our ears that hear the cries, and our will to be obedient to His Word and His purpose for our lives. Dirty hands, tired feet, broken hearts, teary eyes, and listening ears, all combined with humble obedience are some of the qualities of those who are real servants of God.

THE CANDLE

He lit the candle long ago
And He passed it on to me.
I took it from His bloodstained hand
So I could better see.

When He stood beside me on that day
And handed me the light
He said, "You'll keep it burning.
Always have Me in your sight.
For there are those who'll try real hard
To put you in the dark.
They'll try to take away the flame.
They'll stab you in the heart.

"Take this light I've given you
And give it to the world.
Show every man and woman.
Show every boy and girl.
They live in darkness every day
Without this light from Me.
You pass it on to all of them
So then their eyes will see."

But, Lord, am I the one You chose?
Are You giving it to me?
Do You think that I can pass it on
To others who cannot see?
What if I fall and drop it
Or let the flame go out?
I'm not strong enough to keep it lit.
What if I blow it out?

But will You give a new one
If I ruin the one I hold?
Why did You give it to me, Lord?
I don't think I'm very bold.

What did You say? That it's okay?
That the flame will not go out?
That if I fall, You'll catch me.
That's what You're all about.
I'm not so sure I trust myself.
I don't know why You do.
But if it means You love me
Then that is what I'll do.

Sometimes the flame would flicker
But it never would go out.
It lit my path and showed me truth
And took away my doubt.
When I was happy, it was bright
But brighter even still
Was the flame that keeps on burning
When my eyes with tears would fill.

This candle that keeps on shining
Didn't come from earth below.
It came from God our Father
And from Him received its glow.
This light that I am holding
Will keep me ever near
The Spirit of our Father
Through Jesus who is so dear.

This light that's everlasting
Will shine forevermore
To help us through our darkest hour
And lead to heaven's door.

This light will burn eternally
As long as you believe.
His light is everlasting
For salvation, you will receive.

IT WAS GOD

I didn't think it was God
Who called me. It was you.
You called and asked me to serve.
What did I want to do?
I didn't stop to consider
Who I was called to be.
I just said, "Yes, I will."
Someone needed me.

I wasn't prepared for this task.
Much harder than I thought.
With each time I was doing it
His guidance and comfort
I sought.
He gave me others to help me
Along this stressful way.
I wanted to quit many times
But He was telling me, "Stay!"

This journey of serving was long.
The trying of new ways, deep.
I had never thought this way.
I lost a lot of sleep.
Nothing seemed to change.
No progress being made.
One year turned into the next.
I wished I had not stayed.

But one day, something happened.
It came right out of the blue.
"They need your help so much.
This really is not about you."
I had to reassess.

Why had I chosen this?
Was a task so hard from God?
Was there something I had missed?

The Lord was changing me
From the inside, making me pure.
I heard His voice and didn't doubt.
This time, I was sure.
The days turned into months.
The months turned into years.
I surely felt His hand in this
Even though I saw through tears.

We changed. All of us.
Week by week, we tried.
It was getting easier.
More smiles and less we cried.
God was in this from the start.
He called me out. He knew my heart.
Why would He want me to stay at home
When there are others so much alone?

We're pressing on with greater hope.
He's taught me much and helped me cope.
He's opened my eyes and given me light.
Our future
   is
      very
         bright!

HAS THE LORD SPOKEN LATELY?

Has the Lord God spoken lately
To your heart and to your head?
Sometimes we know we hear Him,
Not listening to what He said.
At other times, He speaks
In ways we do not know.
We think it's just another day
But in silence, He calls below.

The Lord is up to something
We truly cannot see.
He is putting things in motion
So someone can be free.
He is using us in ways
We do not understand.
Putting us in places
According to His plan.

A chance encounter at the store
Someone we do not know
The one behind us in the line
Someone without the glow.
A friend we have not seen
Or talked with for a while
Someone near us as we walk
A loner who needs a smile.

Perhaps the Lord is placing us
Close to the ones who're blue
They want a caring heart and ear
Sometimes there are so few.
The Lord will speak to open hearts
It's hard to just believe

He knows it all, whether big or small,
We really can't perceive.

Why do we meet these people?
Can we cause these things to be?
God works in ways mysterious
Unknown to you and me.

Be Faithful, My Child

Be faithful, my child,
For this, you were made
From the time of your birth
To the time of the grave.
I have plans and purposes
That you know nothing about.
Be faithful, my child,
Get up and step out.

To walk on the water
Takes faith in me.
The waves can't distract
If your eyes can only see
My grace and My power
Which give you My peace.
Let go of your fears
And feel the release.

I know where you are.
I know where you've been.
I see now your future.
I've forgiven your sin.
I'm able to do
What's impossible for you.
All it takes is your faith.
I make all things new.

Am I weak and helpless?
Or mighty and great?
Can I see things you don't?
Do I do things too late?

Remember the cross
Where I died for your sin.
Remember My power
That lives deep within.
Remember the tomb
That I left behind.
Remember resurrection.
This will ease your mind.

I live today
To bring you peace.
I rose from the grave
So your worries would cease.
Be filled with My Spirit,
With courage and with truth.
Speak boldly for Me,
To the old and the youth.

I can do all things
I create them anew.
I trust you, My child.
Will you trust Me too?

The Gift That You Have

The gift that you have
The gift that you bring
Is it wisdom or laughter?
Can you teach? Do you sing?
Some are very generous.
Others can heal.
Another can prophesy.
The Spirit will fill
All of God's people
With gifts we can use
To help one another.
We have no excuse.

The Spirit will give us
Abilities to serve
A message of knowledge
To see around the curve.
But none of it counts
If it's not done with heart.
These gifts are from God
We all have our part
Seeing and listening
Leading by faith
Giving to the poor
Not making them wait.

These gifts are not given
To bury or to hide.
They're used to help others
And the Spirit will guide
Bringing to mind
The one who will need
The gift that we have.

Why let them bleed?
So love all the people
And use what you have
The gift that God's given
That will make Him glad
If it's used in service
To God and to man
Bringing faith, hope, and love
To all in this land.

DREAMS

Have you ever had
   a dream so big?
You always thought it
    fine.
Did you let it go
And feel the sting
Of leaving it behind?

Did your dream continue
   through the years
And follow you
   in time?
It was always in
Your heart and soul
And pressing on your mind.

Can you try again
   just one more time?
Push through once more
   with hope.
You can pick it up
And persevere.
He'll show you how to cope.

We're followers of
   the Risen Lord.
His Spirit
   lives within.
We can do all things
With His great power
And dream our dreams again.

When the dreams
    they are impossible,
When the dreams
    they seem too much,
Lift them up to Him.
Let Him give you strength.
Have faith and don't give up.

THE CAMOUFLAGED ONES

Many are the things
We cannot see.
Are we blind or is it
A big mystery?
Like a squirrel
Camouflaged in a tree.
Like a deer in the woods
Or a snake in the grass.
We move along quickly
Too often, we pass
And don't notice what's there
Hidden from our eyes.
If we slow down and look
Oh, what a surprise!
Something in disguise.

Too busy, in a rush,
Much to do and to be
Many places to go
In our community
Why look and observe
What's not red, blue, or gold,
If it's muted and silenced
Not loud and not bold.
Oh, what a surprise.
Something quiet there lies.

There are people in the world
God wants us to view
In the home, in the school,
In the community. That's true.
In the workplace or ballfield
In the market or the pew

In the restaurant or the street
A person with no clue.
Oh, what a surprise.
In silence are their cries.

Through the grace of the Lord
He opens our eyes
To the camouflaged ones
And what a great prize.
The things He reveals
The mysteries He shows
The soul in the darkness
Or the Spirit that glows
Oh, what a surprise.
Something in their eyes.

O Lord, are You camouflaged
When we don't see You there?
You are present in the world
In life everywhere.
We think You're invisible
But we feel You are near.
You are with us, beside us,
Even when it's not clear
In the men and the women
In the girls and the boys
In the laughter and tears
In the sadness and joys.
We don't always show
How we feel in our heart
So much we will hide
That's tearing us apart.
It's not a surprise.
It's observed in our sighs.

O Lord, slow us down.
We need to believe
There are hidden things daily
We just can't conceive
In the people and places
In the dirt and the pain
In the sorrow and loneliness
If we lose or we gain.
Oh, what a surprise.
Someone in disguise.

Scripture about Servanthood and Call

The master was full of praise. "Well done, my good and faithful servant. You have been faithful in handling this small amount, so now I will give you many more responsibilities. Let's celebrate together!"

—Matthew 25: 21

Anyone who wants to be my disciple must follow me, because my servants must be where I am. And the Father will honor anyone who serves me.

—John 12:26

And since I, your Lord and Teacher, have washed your feet, you ought to wash each other's feet.

—John 13:14

You must have the same attitude that Christ Jesus had. Though he was God, he did not think of equality with God as something to cling to. Instead, he gave up his divine privileges; he took the humble position of a slave and was born as a human being.

—Philippians 2:5–7

And having chosen them, he called them to come to him. And having called them, he gave them right standing with himself. And having given them right standing, he gave them his glory.

—Romans 8:30

But to those called by God to salvation, both Jews and Gentiles, Christ is the power of God and the wisdom of God.

—1 Corinthians 1:24

There are different kinds of service, but we serve the same Lord.

—1 Corinthians 12:5

A spiritual gift is given to each of us so we can help each other.

—1 Corinthians 12:7

Therefore, I, a prisoner for serving the Lord, beg you to live a life worthy of your calling, for you have been called by God.

—Ephesians 4:1

Don't repay evil for evil. Don't retaliate with insults when people insult you. Instead, pay them back with a blessing. That is what God has called you to do, and he will bless you for it.

—1 Peter 3:9

God has given each one of you a gift from his great variety of spiritual gifts. Use them well to serve one another.

—1 Peter 4:10

A servant of the Lord must not quarrel but must be kind to everyone, be able to teach, and be patient with difficult people.

—2 Timothy 2:24

Then the righteous ones will reply, "Lord, when did we ever see you hungry and feed you? Or thirsty and give you something to drink? Or a stranger and show you hospitality? Or naked and give you clothing? When did we ever see you sick or in prison and visit you?" And the King will say, "I tell you the truth, when you did it to one of the least of these my brothers and sisters, you were doing it to me!"

—Matthew 25:37–40

CHAPTER 7

THE JOURNEY OF DOUBT, FEAR, AND WORRY

Empty Your Heart
I Am Weary
If I Can't Have the Answer
Living by the Promises
Scripture about Doubt, Fear, and Worry

The journey of doubt, fear, and worry is one that all of us will travel many times during our lives. Life does not always go as planned. Our plans. Life does not always happen when we want it to happen. Our timeline. We are disappointed and frustrated and tired of waiting. Our love is not returned. Our goals are never met. We lose sight of God's plan and purpose for our lives. Maybe we believe He has forgotten about us and has left us out in the cold. We are not sure of ourselves or of Him. And we wonder why God doesn't just step in and take over and relieve us of this misery.

When we doubt, we become like many who walked closely with Jesus. We become like Peter who walked on the water when he had his eyes on the Lord. But when he looked at the waves, he began to sink. We become like Thomas who only believed what he could see with his eyes and touch with his hands. We become like John the Baptist who was in prison and sent the disciples to ask Jesus, "Are you the Messiah we've been expecting, or should we keep looking for someone else?" (Matthew 11:2). In our doubt, we may begin to confront the crisis we are facing and ask the important questions we have never asked. In seeking the answers, our faith may be increased.

When we are fearful, it's because we can't see beyond our horizon. We are scared because we cannot know the future and where our circumstances may take us. We are frightened because of the physical and emotional pain that will not cease. We are undone when death is near, and we have no answers. When we run out of time, energy, and money, we are at the last strand of our rope barely hanging on, and we are terrified because we have finally come to the end of what we can do. Fear can lead us back to the One who knows the future and can give us peace. Our fears may increase our faith and cause us to depend more on Jesus and less on ourselves.

When we worry, we look too much at tomorrow and what might or might not happen. Jesus said, "So, don't worry about tomorrow, for tomorrow will bring its own worries. Today's trouble is enough for today" (Matthew 6:34). When we are anxious, it's because we are not in control. When we are in over our heads, we must turn back to the One who can and will help. Philippians 4:6–7 tells us what to do, "Don't worry about anything; instead, pray about everything. Tell God what you need, and thank him for all he has done. Then you will experience God's peace, which exceeds anything you can understand. His peace will guard your hearts and your minds as you live in Christ Jesus."

Doubt, fear, and worry are a part of our lives. And Jesus knew we would feel these feelings. Why do we think He preached and taught about these things so much? It's because He knows how we are. We are imperfect sinners saved only by the grace of God and those who need a Savior to rescue them from the troubles of this life. Often, we must admit we are the weak, helpless, and frightened little lambs who need the Shepherd. And that's why He died. To be our Shepherd and Savior in the best of times and in the worst of times. Our journey would not be complete, a victorious Christian one, if we always had the solution and never needed our Savior. Our doubts, our fears, and our worries can ultimately draw us closer to Him.

So what is the real answer for these problems? We are to trust and depend on our Father God in every circumstance of life and have faith in His promises in His Holy Word. Yes, He knows how we are and is merciful and gracious toward us. But His real hope and desire for each of us is that we would trust in Him with all our hearts, no matter what happens.

EMPTY YOUR HEART

"Empty your heart,"
He said to me.
"Empty your heart
And let it be.
There's so much stuff
That's deep inside.
Get it out."
I began to cry.

My heart was full
Of things that day,
Things that were getting
In the way
Of my personal relationship
With my Lord.
His voice was speaking
And cut like a sword.

My life had gotten
Too busy, you see—
Too busy with what
Was worrying me.
I'd been in this war
Again and again.
The battle was starting.
Would I win?

The enemy was ready
To pounce on me.
It had happened before
And I could not see.
The enemy wore a
Good disguise.
How would I know
What was truth or lies?

Is this what's really
Happening to me?
Why can't I be happy
And just carefree?
Why not someone else
This time?
I'd been through this war.
I'd committed no crime.

The fear had already
Gotten to my soul.
The devil had grabbed me
And made me cold.
Why should I fear?
What can he do?
He can lie and deceive
And accuse me too.

But I don't have
To listen to him.
He's done this before
And will try it again.
The Lord is my strength
And I will not fear.
The Lord is beside me
And always near.

I know the truth
And it lives in me.
I'm born again
And strong I can be.
No more prison
To shut me out.
No more deception.
I have to shout!

The Lord reigns
In my life today.
He rules and His power
Has not gone away.
He's stronger and mightier
Than all of hell.
He's standing beside me
And I know that well.

I won't be defeated.
This I know.
I talked to the Lord
And He told me so.
All I have to do
Is stand and see.
The Lord will fight
This battle for me.

My heart is empty
Of all my fears.
I'm better now.
I've cried some tears.
I was once afraid
And would not speak.
But now I'm brave
And not so weak.

I'm on His side
And He's with me.
His arm is strong.
His eyes can see.
His voice will speak
And I'll tune my ear.
He'll make me safe.
He's always here.

I Am Weary

I am weary.
I am worn.
I am teary.
I am torn.
I am drowning
    in this desert
    of fears.

You are strong.
You are true.
You're my Savior
And that's who
I can trust
    when I cannot
    go on.

Give me life.
Give me peace.
Give me hope,
Sweet release
From these chains
    that oppress
    my soul.

You are mighty.
You are King.
My deliverer
My everything
I will rest
    in the arms
    of Your love.

IF I CAN'T HAVE THE ANSWER

If I can't have the answer, Lord,
I can have You.
If I can't see the way yet
You can speak truth.
If the pain will not leave
If the birth not conceive
I can choose to have faith
And believe.

If the way is not clear, Lord,
I can still hear Your voice.
If the future looks dim, God,
I can still make a choice.
If the chaos is still here
If the night brings me fear
I can listen and know You
Are near.

If my patience is stretched through this wait
If the steps are slow and it's late
I can still carry on
Even though it is long
Because God is always right and never wrong.

If the sun isn't bright every day
If the rainstorms bring clouds my way
I'll remember the Son
The Holy One
And the race I'll be able to run.

Living by the Promises

Living by the promises
Of Jesus, my Lord,
In every season, every hour,
I have my reward:
Eternal life, eternal love,
The forgiveness of sin.
I have opened my heart
And let the Savior come in.

His promises are many,
The kind he will keep.
He's with me in daylight
And when I'm asleep.
He will never leave me.
He's always by my side
To lead and instruct me,
Forever my guide.

Whenever I'm worried
And living in fear,
I call on His name
And quickly He's near.
He speaks to my heart
And listens to my soul.
He brings me great peace,
Warms me in the cold.

How do I know
Of these promises so true?
They're the ground I stand on.
His words are like glue.
They keep me together
When I'm falling apart.

They penetrate my mind
And remain in my heart.

His promises are found
In the Holy Word of God,
The Bible, the scriptures,
The path we have trod.
If we live by His promises,
We'll have a great light
To shine in the shadows,
To make our days bright.

Jesus, our Savior,
Speaks words to impart
His holiness, His love,
The grace from His heart.
His words are His promises
That share what is true,
Always and forever,
For me and for you.

Scripture about Doubt, Fear, and Worry

So be strong and courageous! Do not be afraid and do not panic…For the LORD your God will personally go ahead of you. He will neither fail you nor abandon you…Do not be afraid or discouraged, for the Lord will personally go ahead of you. He will be with you; he will neither fail you nor abandon you.

—Deuteronomy 31:6,8

God is our refuge and strength, always ready to help in times of trouble.

—Psalm 46:1

My health may fail, and my spirit may grow weak, but God remains the strength of my heart; he is mine forever.

—Psalm 73:26

Trust in the LORD with all your heart; do not depend on your own understanding. Seek his will in all you do, and he will show you which path to take.

—Proverbs 3:5–6

See, God has come to save me. I will trust in him and not be afraid. The Lord God is my strength and my song; he has given me victory.

—Isaiah 12:2

Don't be afraid, for I am with you. Don't be discouraged, for I am your God. I will strengthen you and help you. I will hold you up with my victorious right hand.

—Isaiah 41:10

Do not be afraid, for I have ransomed you. I have called you by name; you are mine. When you go through deep waters, I will be with you. When you go through rivers of difficulty, you will not drown. When you walk through the fire of oppression, you will not be burned up; the flames will not consume you. For I am the Lord, your God, the Holy One of Israel, your Savior.

—Isaiah 43:1c–3a

I am leaving you with a gift—peace of mind and heart. And the peace I give is a gift the world cannot give. So don't be troubled or afraid.

—John 14:27

For I can do everything through Christ, who gives me strength.
—Philippians 4:13

I wait quietly before God, for my victory comes from him. He alone is my rock and my salvation, my fortress where I will never be shaken.

—Psalm 62:1–2

Show me the right path, O Lord; point out the road for me to follow. Lead me by your truth and teach me, for you are the God who saves me. All day long I put my hope in you.

—Psalm 25:3–4

Then Jesus said, "Come to me all of you who are weary and carry heavy burdens, and I will give you rest."

—Matthew 11:28

CHAPTER 8

THE JOURNEY OF SEASONS

What season do you find yourself in right now? We can consider the seasons of nature as a starting point. Spring. Summer. Fall. Winter. These certain times of the year relate well to where we are in our lives. Each stage has certain rhythms, colors, sounds, sights, and smells. We can see ourselves in the trees, the flowers, the skies, the animals, and in all of creation as their actions portray what we are experiencing. In our seasons, we are blooming, growing, and producing. We are changing, dying, and waiting. And then one day, blooming again. We remember that this is a journey. We don't stay in the same place forever. And God is with us.

Consider another journey of the seasons—the spiritual journey. That's another way of looking at our lives. Ecclesiastes 3:1 says, "For everything there is a season, a time for every activity under heaven." This passage in the Bible goes on to name some of the seasons we will travel in and through as we walk the path of life. Some named are birth, death, weeping, laughing, silence, and speaking. Some other seasons in the spiritual life are rebirth, renewal, resurrection, doubt, darkness, and fear. Some of these are colorful and bright like the spring daisies and daffodils. Others are cold, hard, and isolating like the ice of winter. We remember this is a journey. We don't stay in the same season forever, and God is with us in every one of them.

Of course, some stages or seasons of life's journey correspond to our age: child, youth, young adult, middle-aged adult, senior citizen, or whatever category you choose to name it. These are specifically age related, and all have a few common characteristics that go along with them. But age does not necessarily define who a person is or what season they live in. We remember this is a journey. We don't stay the same age forever. We grow and mature with God's grace.

Whatever our circumstances, they can be viewed through the lens of a seasonal journey, a time with a beginning and an ending which leads to the next season and the next path that awaits us. These seasonal travels may seem to last a short period or may continue for what feels like forever. Everyone experiences their own unique time scheme in the number of days, months, or years of duration. This is life. It is a journey of many seasons.

CHANGING COLORS

As I look at the autumn tree
   in front of me,
I see the hand of God.
This tree that has been filled
   with only green leaves
     is beginning to change.
Only God can make it change.
Some leaves at the top are now
   reddish,
   orangish,
   yellowish.
A few weeks ago, they were all green.
Only God can change the colors
   of a tree.
Did He come at night
   and paint the leaves?

I've seen this before.
It happens every fall,
   year after year.
But somehow
   it's different today.
Maybe I am like that tree.
Maybe God is changing my colors.
Perhaps the Lord is changing me
   from a common, ordinary tree
to one that is colorful and beautiful.
Is this my season
   to show the beauty of God
     that has lived
       deep inside my soul?

I wonder if the tree
    knows and senses the change
        from deep within
or if only others can see the outer beauty
    and the colors from the Lord.
Only the One who creates
    can make this change.

The changing colors
    are a sign of God's power
        to transform
something ordinary,
into something colorful
    and bright
    and beautiful.

I am that tree.
God is changing me.

Spring Is Here

Spring is here!
Beauty and color fill our world.
Nature is abuzz with baby birds
    and bumblebees.
Flowers bloom and grow
    and consume us
    with their ever-present
    fragrance.
Spring is here!

It took a while for spring to come.
Winter was as slow as a turtle,
    plodding along in no big
    hurry.
But winter left when it was time
    for it to leave.
I couldn't make it go away.
My wishes could not ease
    the heavy burden of the cold
      and the glacial ground
        under my feet.
Winter would not leave
    before its time.

Spring is here!
It's what I have waited for
    all these long days and weeks
    and months.
Maybe years.

The time has come for
    the earth to be resurrected
    and alive once again.
The colors breathe life into
    our souls once more as we
    recuperate from the dead of
    winter.

The world is beautiful in purples and
    whites and pinks.
No more dull, drab, lifeless, leafless
    season for me.
My eyes are open.
My ears are attentive.
I smell the perfume of nature
    all around me.

My senses are filled every moment
    with this renewal of life.
It is a life that is available
    and a gift to all who observe and
      who embrace the change
        that only God could create
          right before our eyes.
Spring is here!

Seasons of Life

Seasons come and go
    in a certain order and rhythm
        in nature.
We know and recognize these seasons
    by what we see happening
        with our eyes and what we
            remember in our bodies
            and souls.
Multicolored leaves come in glory
    bringing a rainbow of sorts to our
        surroundings. Soon they fall to the
        ground.
Shivery weather appears
    and with it the frost and chilly icebergs.
        Warmth is a precious luxury.
Greenery and spectacular blooms
    come back! We see buds of promise
        even before they return in full.
The brilliant sun and carefree days
    are here. Gardens, tomatoes, roses
        once more! Peaches, pickles,
            peppers.
Things that were deathlike come back. Growth appears.
    The outside world changes
    and sunshine fills our inner being!

We know the cycles of nature
    and have endured the deep freeze
    and the comatose state
    because we realize that it
    won't last forever. We understand
    another season is on the way.
Winter always departs.

Spring and summer
    eventually return.
        Autumn is near.
God made it this way, and
    it doesn't change.
Seasons are from the Lord.
One season always prepares us
    for the next.

Our lives are like the seasons
    but not as predictable.
Some seasons seem to last for years
    and others for only moments.
The seasons of our lives are not
    set in stone.
They do not always come
    when we expect them.
We are not ready
    and do not welcome
    the dead brown grass
        the barren landscape,
        the isolation and bleakness.
But somehow we survive,
    knowing it will change
        one day.
Another season will come
    soon.

The Holy Word of God says,
"There is a time for everything,
    and a season
    for every activity
    under heaven."[1]

[1.] Ecclesiastes 3:1 (NIV)

God's seasons in nature show us
    life and death,
   representing our
   laughter and tears,
examples of our dancing and grieving,
   our words and our silence,
   the love and hate we experience
   in times of peace and war.

In our seasons of life,
   we will love and laugh, rejoice and sing
     with the radiant beams from the sky
      and the floral bouquets of God's
       garden. Our season of joy.
We will struggle and cry,
   endure and persist, growing stronger
   through the cold and the change.
    Our season of tears.
And we will live with hope
   throughout all the seasons of our life
   here which will cease one day…
   and continue in a perfect, peaceful,
   fruitful, glorious season that
    will never end. Amen!

THE LATE OCTOBER TREE

I'm looking at that tree
    God planted years ago.
At the moment, it is
    the late October tree.
It's the tree in my line of sight
    every day.
Today I don't think
    I like what I see.
A portion of the autumn foliage
    that dressed this tree is gone.
Part of the leaves have disappeared
    no longer in sight.
This portion of the tree is
    without its lovely coverings.
It's now an empty spot. Bald.

But the remainder of the tree
    is still full.
The leaves are not as vibrant
    or colorful as they once were
    but they are still there.
Some gold.
Some scarlet.
Some brown.
And other varying shades
    that have faded somewhat.
I know one day the leaves
    will all be gone.
The tree will be like a giant stick
empty branches and distorted limbs.

This is life.
We can't be beautiful
    all the time.
Sooner or later
    our beauty fades and
we easily blend into the other
parts of God's creation.
Will we be beautiful again?
Will we allow God
    to do His work
in this season of rest
    and silence
        and nakedness?

Under all those beautiful leaves
    is the soul of the tree.
Without the branches
    there could be no leaves.
Perhaps there exists a deeper strength
    and courage in the bare tree
    that was not evident at first glance.
The leafless tree represents
    endurance, perseverance, hope,
        and faith in the midst of the changing
            seasons and times in our lives when we
                are without
            what we once held near.
This creation will continue to grow
    without its gorgeous clothes.

Waiting is hard when I don't have what I
    need.
I don't like to be uncovered and
    vulnerable, undressed, and without
        my leaves.
I don't want to be empty. Without.
But the wind keeps blowing
    my leaves away, a few more every day.
Winter is coming soon.

But my hope is not in myself
    or in my beautiful leaves.
My hope is in the One who created me
    and knows my seasons.
He loves me even when I have lost all that I
    thought was mine.

Come, O wind of God, and blow.
Take all my beautiful leaves
    and use them for Your glory.
I will be beautiful again one day.

Scripture about Seasons

Then God said, "Let lights appear in the sky to separate the day from the night. Let them be signs to mark the seasons, days, and years."

—Genesis 1:14

They are like trees planted along the riverbank, bearing fruit each season. Their leaves never wither, and they prosper in all they do.

—Psalm 1:3

The glory of the young is their strength; the gray hair of experience is the splendor of the old.

—Proverbs 20:29

Don't let anyone think less of you because you are young. Be an example to all believers in what you say, in the way you live, in your love, your faith, and your purity.

—1 Timothy 4:12

He has made everything beautiful in its time. He has also set eternity in the hearts of men; yet they cannot fathom what God has done from beginning to end.

—Ecclesiastes 3:11 (NIV)

Don't let the excitement of your youth cause you to forget your Creator. Honor him in your youth before you grow old.

—Ecclesiastes 12:1

Seventy years are given to us! Some even live to be eighty. But the best years are filled with pain and trouble; soon they disappear and we fly away...Teach us to realize the brevity of life, so that we may grow in wisdom...Satisfy us each morning with your unfailing love, so we may sing for joy to the end of our lives.

—Psalm 90:10, 12, 14

But the godly will flourish like palm trees and grow strong like the cedars of Lebanon. For they are transplanted to the Lord's own house. They flourish in the courts of God. Even in old age they will still produce fruit; they will remain vital and green.

—Psalm 92:12–14

When I was a child, I spoke and thought and reasoned as a child. But when I grew up, I put away childish things. Now we see things imperfectly, like puzzling reflections in a mirror, but then we will see everything with perfect clarity. All that I know now is partial and incomplete, but then I will know everything completely, just as God now knows me completely.

—1 Corinthians 13:11–12

So let's not get tired of doing what is good. At just the right time we will reap a harvest of blessings if we don't give up.

—Galatians 6:9

And the one sitting on the throne said, "Look, I am making everything new!" And he also said, "It is finished! I am the Alpha and the Omega, the Beginning and the End."

—Revelation 21:5a, 6a

CHAPTER 9

THE JOURNEY OF LONELINESS, SUFFERING, AND PAIN

If I Share in His Joy
He's Loving Me from the Cross
Forsaken
I Am Looking
Scripture about Loneliness, Suffering, and Pain

This part of our journey should come as no surprise. All of life is not easy, fun, or joyful for Christians or anyone else. The truth in life is that it is hard, tiring, and isolating sometimes in the stages and ages we go through. Darkness and emptiness seem to cloud up our days and ways. Loneliness creeps into our bones and settles down upon us like the plague. Things just happen that we don't expect. Changes take place, monumental ones that we can't control or fix. We are disappointed, and we experience failure. We or our loved ones become sick and disabled. Death comes to those we love. Dementia happens. Couples divorce. Family or close friends move away. Or maybe we're the one moving, leaving behind all we know. Loss and change are not what we want, but it is inevitable. Will we ever be okay again? Our faith in Jesus tells us we will be, but it will take time.

The journey of suffering and pain is like this. It may be physical, emotional, or spiritual. No one goes through life without some form of suffering and pain. It's a part of who we are as humans living in an imperfect world with imperfect people. Perhaps the depth of this suffering is intense, has lasted such a long time, and has caused us to be hopeless. But don't give up. Your journey is not over yet, and Jesus has the last word on everything. Miracles can and do happen in our situations. Or He gives us the strength and wisdom we need to get through whatever it is. Sometimes the end of our suffering and pain means we or our loved ones go home to be with Jesus where none of this exists anymore. We can trust Him who knows and sees it all from His eternal perspective and walks with us, hand in hand.

Remembering the words Jesus spoke to his disciples as He was preparing them for His crucifixion and death may help in this time of isolation, depression, torment, and fear. Jesus knew what was going to take place, but they did not. The worst thing that could possibly happen to their Lord, in their eyes, was about to happen. They would be devastated to put it mildly. Troubled beyond measure and scared beyond belief. So He prepared them in this way and said, "Do not let your hearts be troubled. Trust in God; trust also in me…I am the way and the truth and the life…and I will ask the Father, and He will give you another Counselor to be with you forever—the Spirit of truth. But you know Him, for He lives with you and will be in you. I will not leave you as orphans; I will come to you. Because I live, you also will live. Peace I leave with you; my peace I give you. I do not give to you as the world gives. Do not let your hearts be troubled and do not be afraid" (John 14:1, 6, 16–19, 27 NIV). He was the one who would suffer excruciating, brutal, cruel pain with whips, thorns, and nails on the cross, but He offered His disciples words of comfort and hope. This is the One we call Savior. He understands our rejection, suffering, and pain.

But the best part of the story and the reason for our hope is what happened three days later when Jesus rose from the dead. Of course, no one was looking for this! Dead men are dead and stay that way here on earth. But not Jesus. He was resurrected to life again to bring light, hope, and life to all who believe. In John 8:12, He said, "I am the light of the world. If you follow Me, you won't have to walk in darkness, because you will have the light that leads to life." May His light come into your life today.

Whatever you are facing at this moment that has caused suffering, pain, and loneliness is something that many others have experienced. You are not alone. Pray. Ask the Lord to put you in touch with someone who has lived through a similar situation, someone kind and loving who can walk with you at this time and be your friend. Hope lives in the hearts of believers who can share their testimony and how Jesus was and still is present with them today.

If I Share in His Joy

If I share in His joy
I will share in His pain.
It's not either but both
For His love will remain.

In His joy, I'm immersed
In a shower of care.
I experience the fulfillment
Of heavenly prayer.
I hear angels; they're singing
In praise of His name.
I feel peace in my soul
And delight in His reign.

In His pain, I'm subjected
To things here on earth
That make me then break me
And take all my worth.
I am crushed and rejected
And left in the cold.
I'm alone and dejected,
Not a hand left to hold.

I don't have a choice
Of His joy or His pain
If I want to reach heaven,
Where eternity I gain.
It's not either but both
If I give Him my life.
He will give me His joy
And hold on in my strife.
He'll never forsake me.
He's always right there.
In His joy, I'll have strength
So His burdens I can bear.

HE'S LOVING ME FROM THE CROSS

I sit and pray.
I ask and weep.
I follow in
My Savior's feet.
I try to do
The things I can.
I try to please
The Lord, not man.
I bring my doubts
And all my fears.
I cry for help
And shed my tears.
I give and serve.
I pray and teach.
I offer hope.
Sometimes I preach.
But still I feel
So far away
From God, My Father,
And His holy way.
I feel alone.
I have no peace.
I've lost my joy.
Why did it cease?

I look above,
See what I've lost.
He's loving me
From the cross.

He listens carefully
To what I say.
He talks to me

Every day.
He gives me hope
And gifts of love.
He's closer than
A tight-fitting glove.
He intervenes
And provides for me.
He protects my soul
And helps me see.

He's with me
Through the day and night.
He hears me laugh.
He sees my fright.

He wants the best.
He gives me life.
He gives me words
That cut like a knife.
He offers forgiveness
And a helping hand.
He has promised eternity
In the heavenly land.
He's love and peace.
He's joy and truth.
He brings me freedom.
My chains He will loose.
He looks down from heaven.
He's by my side.
He lives each day.
For me He died.

When I see my Savior,
I count the cost.
He's loving me
From the cross.

FORSAKEN

When all your friends forsake you
And you don't have any hope
When your burdens are too much
And so heavy is your yoke
When you feel the teardrops falling
And they never seem to stop
When your heart is shattered to pieces
And you feel like such a flop
It's then you'll turn to Jesus
Who understands and really cares
It's then you'll feel His hand
And the scars He always wears
It's then you'll know He bled
On the cross at Calvary
It's then you'll see He suffered
Just like you and just like me.

I Am Looking

I am looking for the beautiful
   That happens each day.
For the colorful skies
And bright morning rays
For sweet baby animals
And the birds at play
For the flittering butterfly
As it makes its way

I am looking for the quiet times
   To come to me
In moments when I'm willing
To sit and just be.
The stillness and silence
May somehow set me free
Like the wind that blows
On the billowing sea.

I'm looking for the healing hand
   Just beyond my grasp.
I reach out in my prayers
And I constantly ask.
This is my journey.
This is my task.
I'm looking for the help
And the hope that will last.

I'm looking for peaceful days
    That take away fear.
Sometimes they are far away.
Sometimes they are near.
The anxious weeks pass by
And it's not very clear
If my weak, thin voice
The Lord can really hear.

I am looking for the Holy One
    In the midst of this pain.
I just can't believe this
Would happen again.
I thought it was finished.
I argue and complain.
I feel like I'm left out
In a downpour of rain.

I'm looking for a new day
    That leads to better things.
A day of rejoicing
When my voice really sings.
This time in the future
Is what my Lord brings
With love and with healing
Where His eternity rings.

I am looking for my Jesus.
To Him, I will cling.

SCRIPTURE ABOUT LONELINESS, SUFFERING, AND PAIN

Hear me as I pray, Lord. Be merciful and answer me! My heart has heard you say, "Come and talk with me." And my heart responds, "Lord, I am coming."

—Psalm 27:7–8

The Lord hears his people when they call to him for help. He rescues them from all their troubles. The Lord is close to the broken-hearted; he rescues those whose spirits are crushed.

—Psalm 34:17–18

Do not be afraid, for I have ransomed you. I have called you by name; you are mine. When you go through deep waters, I will be with you. When you go through rivers of difficulty, you will not drown. When you walk through the fire of oppression, you will not be burned up; the flames will not consume you. For I am the Lord, your God, the Holy One of Israel, your Savior.

—Isaiah 43:1b–3a

As the sun went down that evening, people throughout the village brought sick family members to Jesus. No matter what their diseases were, the touch of his hand healed every one.

—Luke 4:40

All praise to God the Father of our Lord Jesus Christ. God is our merciful Father and the source of all comfort. He comforts us in all our troubles so that we can comfort others. When they are troubled, we will be able to give them the same comfort God has given us. For the more we suffer for Christ, the more God will shower us with his comfort through Christ.

—2 Corinthians 1:3–5

Are any of you suffering hardships? You should pray. Are any of you happy? You should sing praises. Are any of you sick? You should call for the elders of the church to come and pray over you, anointing you with oil in the name of the Lord. Such a prayer offered in faith will heal the sick, and the Lord will make you well. And if you have committed any sins, you will be forgiven.

—James 5:13–15

By his wounds you are healed.

—1 Peter 2:24b

But the Lord stood with me and gave me strength so that I might preach the Good News in its entirety for all the Gentiles to hear. And he rescued me from certain death. Yes, and the Lord will deliver me…and will bring me safely into his heavenly Kingdom. All glory to God forever and ever! Amen.

—2 Timothy 4:17–18

O Lord, hear me as I pray; pay attention to my groaning. Listen to my cry for help, my King and my God, for I pray to no one but you. Listen to my voice in the morning, Lord. Each morning I bring my requests to you and wait expectantly.

—Psalm 5:1–3

Yet I am confident I will see the Lord's goodness while I am here in the land of the living. Wait patiently for the Lord. Be brave and courageous. Yes, wait patiently for the Lord.

—Psalm 27:13–14

CHAPTER 10

THE JOURNEY OF SALVATION AND HOLINESS

Holy Communion
The Path of Life
I'm a Flower
Holy Father
Love the Hidden Person
Be Light in their Darkness
Scripture about Salvation and Holiness

The journey of salvation and holiness is what our life in Christ is all about. It begins when we accept Jesus as our personal Savior and invite Him into our heart. This means we are saved, rescued, and delivered from the power of sin and death. In turning to Jesus, we realize that we cannot make it on our own anymore. We conclude that we need the help of someone more powerful and stronger than we are. We see the error of our ways and want to change and become a different person. In confession and repentance, we call on the name of Jesus and ask for mercy and forgiveness. We turn away from the worldly way of living and seek to live the sacred life to which God has called us.

This is only the beginning of our new life in Christ. Many changes will be made as we travel this road with the Lord. When we become a Christian, we start on our journey toward holiness. Now that we have given our lives to the Lord, we become infants and must learn and understand how God our Father wants us to live. It is a long process that takes a lifetime as we become the person God created us to be. He is molding us and making us into the image of His Son Jesus. We are to have the mind of Christ and follow in His footsteps.

Thankfully we have the Holy Spirit, the Spirit of truth, to teach us and guide us along this path of holiness. The Holy Spirit lives within us and will teach us everything and remind us of what Jesus said. The Holy Spirit will convict us of sin as we journey on this pathway. Traveling this road toward holiness does not mean we are expected to be perfect. We are not and will not be until we get to heaven. We are still sinners saved only by the grace of God. But we are not on the pathway toward destruction and evil anymore. We have decided to follow the highway to heaven with Jesus by our side. This is the journey toward holiness. There is so much truth that we do not yet know about God, about ourselves, about our world, and how we are to live in it as members of the family of God. This journey toward holiness will last a lifetime.

Holy Communion

Communion is a time
We are present with the Lord.
We talk. We pray. We sing.
We listen to the Word.
We come to see Him now.
We come to see Him then.
We come to see Him in the midst
Of when He comes again.

His body and His blood
Are what we all partake.
He gave His life for all of us.
He did it for our sake.
The sacrifice He made
Was once, for all mankind.
He did it for the poor.
He did it for the blind.
He gave His life for you.
He gave His life for me
So we would all believe.
From sin, we would be free.

The bread and the wine
Are symbols of His love,
His body, and His blood
Given from above.
As we eat and drink this meal
Let us come upon our knees,
Looking to the Holy One
Who listens to our pleas,

Seeking only Him
Knowing of our sin
Listening for His voice
That lives so deep within.
Praying in His name
Looking for the way
Seeking only truth
And guidance for this day.

We celebrate You now.
You give us all new life.
We thank You for the cross,
Your total sacrifice.
We praise You for this meal.
We thank You for Your love.
We look into tomorrow
For the feast You have above.
For in heaven, You have waiting
A table prepared by Thee
A banquet that is ready
When Your face we know, we'll see.

We see it now, Lord Jesus.
We're ready to partake.
Come fill us with Your Spirit.
Let us eat the bread You make.
Let us drink the wine You pour.
Let us feel Your Presence here.
We open up our hearts and souls.
We want to feel You near.

For in this meal, we give you
Our body and our souls.
We offer You ourselves
All the pieces. Make us whole.
We take the cup. We take the bread.

It fills us with Your love.
Transform us to Your likeness.
Absorb us with Your love.

THE PATH OF LIFE

I walked the path that I had walked
So many times before
The path that as a little girl
Had taken me to the store.
The sidewalks weren't much different
Than when I was a child.
I'd ridden on my bike with friends,
So young and yet so mild.

Now I am grown and not so young
And walked that path again.
I saw the things with different eyes
Looking back at where I'd been.
The trees were there, the flowers too,
And all the homes I'd known.
The families, I knew them well,
And could see how they had grown.

This time, I slowed down on the path
To see how time had passed.
For others, it may have seemed quite slow
But for me, it seemed so fast.
The path that I was walking
I had been on times before
But this time, it had a different feel.
The Lord had something more.

How many had chosen this path
And been where I am now?
Did they stroll with eyes wide open
Or did they run with furrowed brow?

Did they see the things that I have seen?
Did they wave to passersby?
Did the memory of a saint they'd known
Bring a tear to their weary eye?

I wonder if the others who came
Along this pleasant way
Have felt the presence of the Lord
In each and every day?
Did they see Him in the churches
And in the eyes of those they passed?
Did they view His mighty hand of life
In the growing of the grass?

I wonder if my neighbors
Who walked this path before
And have left this earthly life
Have appeared at heaven's door.
Did they recognize the face of God
While they were living here?
Did they know His presence and His love
And want to feel Him near?
For if we cannot see the Lord
On this His land so dear
Will we know Him in the heavens?
After death? It should be clear.

This path that we are walking
Will come to an end one day.
It may be quick or all drawn out.
It may come at work or play.
No one knows the day or hour,
Not why or how or when.
But we know that it is coming…
Can you see where you have been?

Which path we choose to walk on
And how we choose to be
Will determine where we're going
Where we'll spend eternity.
Is the path that you have chosen
The one that's broad and wide?
Or have you chosen the narrow one
With Jesus by your side?

This path that I am walking
I will walk
Again one day
In heaven and in the presence of Him
Who walks with me today.

I'm a Flower

I'm a flower!
Look at me!
I'm so pretty!
Can't you see?
The Lord is working
Deep inside.
I am blooming.
He will provide.

He sends rain
So I can grow.
He sends the Son
So I can know
The light that leads me
Out of pain,
Out of darkness.
No more stain.

I'd been buried
A long, long time.
Only a seed.
No sun could shine.
But now the light
Has come to me.
He's given me hope.
Now I'm free!

I'm a flower!
Can't you see!
I'm in bloom!
This is me.

HOLY FATHER

Holy Father,
Wise and good,
You love us as
Our Creator would.
You give us life,
Take us from sin,
Breathe in us,
And we're born again.
We begin afresh.
We begin anew.
We love You first
And others too.
Our life becomes
A way to be
Your love in the world,
Your hands and feet.
We give of ourselves.
We give of our time.
We give of our money
Not withholding a dime.

As disciples of
The Holy One
We learn to love
Just like the Son.
We spread His truth.
We speak His Word
To those who know
Or have not heard.
We love with cheer
And sacrifice too
For the homeless, the poor,
The least, the few.

We read God's Word.
We talk to Him.
We sing His songs.
He forgives our sin.

He is our Teacher
If we listen with care
To His words and His voice.
Our burdens, He will bear.
The truth is what
He speaks so clear.
He calms our doubt
And removes our fear.
His peace, His love,
His mercy, His grace
Are what we receive
In life, in this race.

The race isn't easy.
It's long and tough.
It's full of surprises
And gets pretty rough.
But the Father provides
All that we need
For this journey of life.
He sees every deed.
We run fast.
We walk slow.
We stop.
We go.
We stumble.
We fall.
We cry.
We call.
One more day
One more hour

One more breath
No more power

The finish line
We'll cross at last.
Our life on earth
Is gone and past.
We look to that day
With hope in our eyes.
We're home at last
In the heavenly skies.

LOVE THE HIDDEN PERSON

Love the hidden person
You cannot see today.
Look beyond their actions
And the words they say.
Be kind and gentle to them.
Remember them when you pray.
Don't leave them in the storm.
Invite them in to stay.

Love the hidden person.
You don't know who they are.
Underneath their appearance
Could be a shining star.
With a helpful, patient spirit
They could probably go far.
Give them some attention
And help them raise the bar.

Love the hidden person.
They have many fears.
They go to bed each night
Crying many tears.
I wonder if they have
Any Christian peers.
Or if their life is filled
With slams and crazy jeers.

Love the hidden person
That lives in your own soul.
Why are you afraid
Of giving up control?

The Holy Spirit power
Helps you to be bold
Encourages you to live by faith
Even when you're old.

Love the hidden person.
We all have one inside
The one who only God knows
The one we try to hide
The one who sings the song
The one who feels the tide
The one who is committed
The one who's on God's side

Love the hidden person
So everyone can see
Beyond the face and eyes
To the one who's really me.
Beneath the outer layer
Is someone who longs to be
A person loved by God and man
Singing a song of victory.

BE LIGHT IN THEIR DARKNESS

Be light in their darkness
For those who can't see.
They don't know the Word
And they don't follow Me.
The road to destruction
Is what they all choose.
Not knowing forgiveness
Is what they will lose.

Be light in their journey.
They don't know the way.
They stumble and fall
Each minute, each day.
How will they know
Of a Savior who cares
If we all pass them by
And they get only stares?

Be light in their prison
Because you are free.
He's spoken to you
And now you can be
A voice and a touch
Bringing them hope.
They are living alone
And don't know how to cope.

Be light in their shadows.
Sometimes just a spark
Will brighten their path
And it won't be so dark.

They need one who's safe
And someone who shows
Our Father is faithful
In our highs and our lows.

If you think back in time
To a faraway place
You'll remember someone
Who showed you His grace.
Your eyes were opened,
Shadows slipped away.
They gave you His message
And taught you to pray.

This brightness you're given
Can't be hidden away.
You're holding His hand.
With you, He will stay.
Not darkness nor death
Can put out His light.
Each moment, each hour
Our future is bright.

Be the beacon that you are
A lighthouse on the sea
Bringing others to the true light
That comes from only Me.

SCRIPTURE ABOUT SALVATION AND HOLINESS

For God loved the world so much that he gave his one and only Son, so that everyone who believes in him will not perish but have eternal life. God sent his Son into the world not to judge the world, but to save the world through him.

—John 3:16–17

Let me state clearly to all of you…that he was healed by the powerful name of Jesus Christ the Nazarene, the man you crucified but whom God raised from the dead…There is salvation in no one else! God has given no other name under heaven by which we must be saved.

—Acts 4:10, 12

Since God chose you to be the holy people he loves, you must clothe yourselves with tenderhearted mercy, kindness, humility, gentleness, and patience. Make allowance for each other's faults and forgive anyone who offends you. Remember, the Lord forgave you, so you must forgive others. Above all, clothe yourselves with love, which binds us all together in perfect harmony.

—Colossians 3:12–14

For God saved us and called us to live a holy life. He did this, not because we deserved it, but because it was his plan before the beginning of time—to show us his grace through Christ Jesus. And now he has made this plain to us by the appearing of Christ Jesus, our Savior. He broke the power of death and illuminated the way to life and immortality through the Good News.

—2 Timothy 1:9–10

For God's will was for us to be made holy by the sacrifice of the body of Jesus Christ, once for all time. For by that one offering he forever made perfect those who are being made holy.

—Hebrews 10:10, 14

And I will ask the Father, and he will give you another Advocate, who will never leave you. He is the Holy Spirit, who leads into all truth.

—John 14:16–17a

But when my Father sends the Advocate as my representative—that is, the Holy Spirit—he will teach you everything and will remind you of everything I have told you.

—John 14:26

But you will receive power when the Holy Spirit comes upon you. And you will be my witnesses, telling people about me everywhere—in Jerusalem, throughout Judea, in Samaria, and to the ends of the earth.

—Acts 1:8

Through the power of the Holy Spirit who lives within us, carefully guard the precious truth that has been entrusted to you.

—2 Timothy 1:14

But when God our Savior revealed his kindness and love, he saved us, not because of the righteous things we had done, but because of his mercy. He washed away our sins, giving us a new birth and new life through the Holy Spirit. He generously poured out the Spirit upon us through Jesus Christ our Savior. Because of his grace he declared us righteous and gave us confidence that we will inherit eternal life.

—Titus 3:4–7

CHAPTER 11

THE JOURNEY OF DEATH, RESURRECTION, AND ETERNAL LIFE

I'm a Butterfly
Death Comes Silently
Through Death
Light at the End
Scripture about Death, Resurrection, and Eternal Life

The journey of death is not one we prefer to discuss. But it comes eventually to everyone who is alive. All of us will die one day. Some live longer than others. Many have a shorter length of time on this earth. We know of those who have died quickly and unexpectedly. There are others whose death was a slow progressive one that lasted for many years. None of us know the day or the time, but we know it is a part of life. We are born, we live, and then one day, we die. No one is immune to death.

When death is paired with resurrection, that paints a different picture altogether. Death is not seen as a finality. The grave is not our eternal home. This life is more than our few years on the planet earth. Death is not the end but a new beginning for those who believe in Jesus Christ as the Son of God, the one who died for us and was resurrected has passed that gift on to all of God's children. Eternal life is ours. We will be with God in the world beyond what any of us know. Resurrection! Eternal life! Forever! Hallelujah!

In the gospel of John, Jesus spoke about the resurrection and eternal life. He said, "For it is my Father's will that all who see his Son and believe in him should have eternal life. I will raise them up at the last day" (John 6:40). And in chapter 11, he spoke more words to clarify our understanding, saying, "I am the resurrection and the life. Anyone who believes in me will live, even after dying" (verse 25).

In John, chapter 14, Jesus spoke again, saying, "Don't let your hearts be troubled. Trust in God, and trust also in me. There is more than enough room in my Father's home. If this were not so, would I have told you that I am going to prepare a place for you? When everything is ready, I will come and get you, so that you will always be with me where I am" (verses 1–3). Resurrection and eternal life!

Death is a passage all will experience. It will lead to resurrection and eternal life forever with Jesus for those who live for Christ. No one can imagine how glorious that will be to live in the holy place with our Holy Father and all the holy saints! Revelation 21:4 tells us, "He will wipe every tear from their eyes, and there will be no more death or sorrow or crying or pain. All these things are gone forever." A new creation! A new heaven and a new earth! A new beginning that is everlasting!

Death comes first then resurrection and eternal life!

I'm a Butterfly

I'm a butterfly!
Now I'm free!
The Spirit of Jesus
Lives in me.
No longer will I crawl
And look at the ground.
I will lift up my eyes,
For I am heaven bound.
I can spread my wings.
I can feel His breath.
I've overcome this life
Through resurrection and death.

I'm a glorious new creature
Colorful and bright.
I've seen His face
And felt His sweet light.
I've come out of the tomb.
I've come out of the grave.
Not bound in the cocoon,
I'm no longer afraid.
I can float up above
All the cares of this earth.
He's given me new life.
Through His death, there's rebirth.

DEATH COMES SILENTLY

Death comes silently,
When no one knows,
How the wind comes,
Where the wind blows.
It comes without warning
In the blink of an eye.
One minute, we're here.
The next, we die.

Death comes silently
In the middle of the night,
When darkness is around
And others out of sight.
Sometimes in a hospital
Sometimes at home
Sometimes with many people
Sometimes alone

Death comes silently
Like a whispering voice.
My name is called.
Will heaven rejoice?
Will the angels in heaven
Rejoice and sing
When I enter the place
Of our God and King?

Death comes silently.
Others will not see
The light from heaven
Shining on me.

They won't see my Savior
Or hear His sweet voice,
But when He calls
I'll have no choice!
I'll leave this earth
And the world behind!
I'm going to glory
Where there's love divine!

Death comes silently
And no one can hear
Only God and the Spirit
And my Jesus are clear
When that day and that moment
Will come to me.
Praise the Lord! Praise the Lord!
His face will I see!

Death comes silently
On earth below
But a great sound is heard
In the place where I go.
I'll dance, and I'll sing!
I'll laugh, and I'll shout!
No more pain! No more sin!
No more fear and doubt!

Death comes silently,
But on my way there,
I'll sing a song
And say a prayer.
Death comes silently
To take me home
To the place where I'll live,
Never alone.

I'll live with my Master
And see all my friends,
The saints who are there
Where life never ends.
I'll live in the presence
Of God and His Son,
The eternal presence,
The Holy One.

Life will be better
Than ever before!
Death comes silently
To open the door.
A new life is waiting
Just beyond this.
Heaven is filled
With love and bliss.

Death comes silently,
This I know,
Life forever after
In the place where I go.
Death comes silently.
I know I'll be blessed
To enter that place
Of eternal rest.
The silence is over.
Now I can hear
The voice of my Savior
Perfectly clear!
The silence is gone!
The world has passed!
Resurrection has come!
Peace at last!

THROUGH DEATH

Through death
God brings us back to Him.
Back to this place
That has no sin.
Where angels fly
And rivers flow,
Where trees are lush
And gardens grow.
The roads are paved
With precious gold
And saints live there,
So we are told.

We see our loved ones
Once again.
Their faces are aglow
For Him.
We have no anger.
We cry no tears.
We are healed of sickness.
We have no fears.
But best of all
We get to see
Our Father, our God,
The Prince of Peace.

We get to live with Him
In this place.
We get to talk to Him
Face-to-face.

What will I ask Him?
How will it be
When I'm in heaven
And can finally see
Our Father, our Savior,
The Son of God,
I can touch Him and feel Him
Be where He has trod.

I can see His light
And touch His hand.
Forever and ever
I'll live in this land.
No, death won't hold us
And neither will sin.
He'll raise us up
So we can live with Him.

LIGHT AT THE END

Finally,
   there's light
   at the end of this
      long tunnel.
Some of us saw the light
   early on.
Our journey was no less tedious
   but perhaps filled with hope
      in the ending and finality of these
        earthly, temporary things.
The end is almost here.
Rejoice at last because in every ending
   there is a new beginning!
The task is almost complete.
The light shines brighter and brighter
   every day.
The burden is being lifted
      and our hearts and minds are being renewed
        once again.
The glorious day will appear
   as it always does
      with weary hearts
        thankful
          for the finish line.
The ending of a journey is much better
   than its beginning,
      so far removed from us now.
The last few miles, the hardest ones,
   will be traveled with feet that are certain
      of their future.
Peace at last and rest for the soul.

Scripture about Death, Resurrection, and Eternal Life

I tell you the truth, those who listen to my message and believe in God who sent me have eternal life. They will never be condemned for their sins, but they have already passed from death into life.

—John 5:24

And this is what God has testified: He has given us eternal life, and this life is in his Son.

—1 John 5:11

And now we live in fellowship with the true God because we live in fellowship with his Son, Jesus Christ. He is the only true God, and he is eternal life.

—1 John 5:20b

It is the same way with the resurrection of the dead. Our earthly bodies are planted in the ground when we die, but they will be raised to live forever. Our bodies are buried in brokenness, but they will be raised in glory. They are buried in weakness, but they will be raised in strength. They are buried as natural human bodies, but they will be raised as spiritual bodies. For just as there are natural bodies, there are also spiritual bodies.

—1 Corinthians 15:42–44

For no one can come to me unless the Father who sent me draws them to me, and at the last day I will raise them up.

—John 6:44

I tell you the truth, anyone who believes has eternal life.

—John 6:47

For since we believe Jesus died and was raised to life again, we also believe that when Jesus returns, God will bring back with him the believers who have died.

—1 Thessalonians 4:14

For we know that when this earthly tent we live in is taken down (that is, when we die and leave this earthly body), we will have a house in heaven, an eternal body made for us by God himself and not by human hands.

—2 Corinthians 5:1

He will give eternal life to those who keep on doing good, seeking after the glory and honor and immortality that God offers.

—Romans 2:7

But now you are free from the power of sin and have become slaves of God. Now you do those things that lead to holiness and result in eternal life. For the wages of sin is death, but the free gift of God is eternal life through Christ Jesus our Lord.

—Romans 6:22–23

And this world is fading away, along with everything that people crave. But anyone who does what pleases God will live forever.

—1 John 2:17

God showed us how much he loved us by sending his one and only Son into the world so that we might have eternal life through him.

—1 John 4:9

CHAPTER 12

THE JOURNEY OF THANKSGIVING AND PRAISE

Thank You for the People
God is Where I Am
You Are the Shade
Forever Thankful
Scripture about Thanksgiving and Praise

For Christians, the journey of thanksgiving and praise should be an everyday way of living. Psalm 100:4–5 says, "Enter his gates with thanksgiving; go into his courts with praise. Give thanks to him and praise his name. For the Lord is good. His unfailing love continues forever, and his faithfulness continues to each generation." How many times have we read in the Bible other passages that tell us these same things? It is the kind of life God intends for us to have, ever grateful for all He has done for us. When we consider God's presence and grace in the past, the present, and the future, thanksgiving and praise should be on our lips constantly.

What causes you to give praise and thanks to God? Some people are blessed with a spirit of thanksgiving and are thankful almost all the time. Others are grateful when prayers are answered or something joyful happens. Many are especially happy to praise the name of the Lord in times of fruitfulness and plenty. When we have good health, better health, or healing we may be eager to offer our thanks to God. At weddings, anniversaries, births, graduations, birthdays, and other special celebrations, we always find an abundance of reasons for our praise. We can recognize His hand at work in our lives and in the lives of all these people at the special times in their lives! We give Him all the glory, honor, and praise!

Praise and thanksgiving are not as easy in unexpected times of difficulty, in hardships, in suffering, and in the trials and tribulations that will come to all people if they live long enough. The journey of life from beginning to end is not just one big party. Everyone goes through hard times. In this part of our journey, we must decide if God is still with us, for us, beside us. We must choose to believe and have faith in who He says He is. We have to trust in His promises, knowing that He is able to make "all things work together for good for those who love God, who are called according to his purpose" (Romans 8:28 NRSV). In all our circumstances, we can offer our praise and thanksgiving for His strength and His faithfulness in walking with us every step of the way. Lamentations 3:22–23 reminds us, "The faithful love of the Lord never ends! His mercies never cease. Great is his faithfulness; his mercies begin afresh each morning." Praise the Lord!

THANK YOU FOR THE PEOPLE

Thank you, O Lord, for the people
You put in my life every day
People to laugh with and play with,
Neighbors who would run and would
play,
Friends who gave of themselves to me,
Spending with me precious time,
Friends who would travel to new places,
Together new mountains, we'd climb.

All through my life are the angels
Who helped in my time of need.
They brought me great love and
comfort,
Were faithful in word and in deed.
They taught me truth from the Bible
And helped me in learning to pray.
Some wiped my tears and calmed my
fears
As I listened and learned to obey.

I wonder if I have done this
For others I've known in my life.
Did I ease their pain and sorrow?
Did I bring about less strife?
I pray I brought them peace and hope
And stayed with them for a while,
Not rushing off to leave them there
And perhaps I made them smile.

O Lord, I'm ever grateful.
You've blessed my life with Your love
Through those who live with me on
earth
And through those in heaven above.
Your grace and mercy come to me
Each day as long as I live.
Thank You, Lord. I've felt your touch
Through people who were willing to
give.

GOD IS WHERE I AM

God is where
I am today
In my work
Along the way
No matter
Where I go
The service
High or low
God is where
I am today.

In cars or in buses
On foot or in planes
On subs or horses
On bikes or trains
God is where
I am today.
God will
Make a way.

In old and young
In middle age
In TV or music
On every page
In science and nature
In church and state
God will
Make a way.

In the desert
Or on the plain
In the snow
Or in the rain
On the mountain
Or by the sea
My God will reveal
Himself to me.

In China, in Africa
In India or Japan
The US or Australia
Or any other land
On faraway islands
In south or in north
God makes His home
And His Spirit comes forth.

God is where
I am today
In my work
Along the way
No matter
Where I go
The service
High or low
God is where
I am today.

YOU ARE THE SHADE

You are the shade.
You are the breeze.
You are the flowers.
You are the trees.
You are the sky.
You are the sea.
You are the sun
    That shines upon me.

You are the night.
You are the rain.
You are the butterflies.
You are the grain.
You are the clouds.
You are the moon.
You are the heavens
    That I'll see pretty soon.

You are the music
That I sing each day.
You are the words
That I use to pray.
You are the fruit
That tastes so sweet.
You are the ground
    Under my feet.

You are my heart.
You are my ears.
You are my hands.
You are my tears.
You are my eyes
Through which I see.
You are my Lord
Who created me.

FOREVER THANKFUL

Lord, I'm thankful for the many times
You touch me; I'm unaware.
You're loving, kind, and gentle.
Your wisdom You always share.
I don't notice Your presence each day
Till I stop to look back and see
You were there when I needed help.
Your hand led and guided me.

I'm grateful for Your holy protection.
You save me when I don't know
There's danger ahead or behind me.
You stop me when I want to go.
Your Word gives me strength to endure.
Your peace lets me sleep at night.
Your Spirit convicts me of sin
Many times when I think I'm right.

You've healed my body through the ages
And given me all of these years.
You've provided the doctors and nurses
And counted all of my tears.
You've given me shelter and clothes,
Each day the food I eat,
A roof for those rainy days,
And shoes for my tired feet

But most of all, knowing Jesus my Lord
Brings praise to these lips of mine.
He's given me abundant life
Which I have throughout all time.
He brings me joy in sadness.
His blood covers all my sin.

He's with me all the hours of day
From the beginning until the end.

Forgive me, Lord, when I forget
To praise You in everything.
In sunny days and stormy ones
I still have a song to sing.
This life on earth isn't all there is.
We're assured of a place of peace.
In the heavenlies, we have a house
When our days down here shall cease.

Thank You, Lord, a million times more
I can't wait to see Your face.
Until that time, sweet Jesus
I rest filled up with Your grace.

Scripture About Thanksgiving and Praise

Let all that I am praise the Lord; with my whole heart I will praise his holy name. Let all that I am praise the Lord; may I never forget the good things he does for me. He forgives all my sins and heals all my diseases. He redeems me from death and crowns me with love and tender mercies. He fills my life with good things. My youth is renewed like the eagle's!

—Psalm 103:1–5

Be thankful in all circumstances, for this is God's will for you who belong to Christ Jesus.

—1 Thessalonians 5:18

Therefore, let us offer through Jesus a continual sacrifice of praise to God, proclaiming our allegiance to his name.

—Hebrews 13:15

Praise the name of God forever and ever, for he has all wisdom and power. He controls the course of world events; he removes kings and sets up other kings. He gives wisdom to the wise and knowledge to the scholars. He reveals deep and mysterious things and knows what lies hidden in the darkness, though he is surrounded by light. I thank and praise you, God of my ancestors, for you have given me wisdom and strength.

—Daniel 2:20–23b

Praise the Lord! Give thanks to the Lord, for he is good! His faithful love endures forever. Who can list the glorious miracles of the Lord? Who can ever praise him enough?

—Psalm 106:1–2

The Lord is your keeper; the Lord is your shade at your right hand.

—Psalm 121:5 NRSV

Praise the Lord! How good to sing praises to our God! How delightful and how fitting!

—Psalm 147:1

All praise to God, the Father of our Lord Jesus Christ, who has blessed us with every spiritual blessing in the heavenly realms because we are united with Christ. Even before he made the world, God loved us and chose us in Christ to be holy and without fault in his eyes.

—Ephesians 1:3–4

So we praise God for the glorious grace he has poured out on us who belong to his dear Son. He is so rich in kindness and grace that he purchased our freedom with the blood of his Son and forgave our sins. He has showered his kindness on us, along with all wisdom and understanding.

—Ephesians 1:7–8

I always thank my God when I pray for you…because I keep hearing about your faith in the Lord Jesus and your love for all of God's people.

—Philemon 4–5

All glory to him who alone is God, our Savior through Jesus Christ our Lord. All glory, majesty, power, and authority are his before all time, and in the present, and beyond all time! Amen.

—Jude 25

CHAPTER 13

THE JOURNEY OF CHRISTMAS

Christmastime
The Tree
Christmas Comes
A Christmas Story
A Quiet Sacred Moment
Scripture about Christmas

The journey of Christmas begins long ago in the past in Bethlehem when God sent His Son to earth to be born in a manger. We know the story all too well. The angels. The shepherds. The stable. Mary and Joseph. The baby, the Son of God. This journey continues into the present day as we worship and adore Him as the Messiah, the One God promised. He is, as John 1:14 tells us, "the Word became flesh and made his dwelling among us" (NIV). He is the One the angels brought good news about. "Today in the town of David a Savior has been born to you; he is Christ the Lord" (Luke 2:11 NIV). He is the One God sent because He loved the world so much. As John 3:16 tells us, "For God so loved the world that He gave his one and only Son, that whoever believes in Him shall not perish but have eternal life" (NIV). This is Christmas. The gift of life eternal through Jesus.

The journey of Christmas continues into our future when the kingdom of God will be realized by all people. Those who have accepted and received the gift of Christmas, Jesus Christ who was born in a manger, died on the cross, and was resurrected on the third day, will live eternally with God in the heavens forever and ever. This gift is what makes our life worth living. Jesus is the gift of the past, the present, and the future. Don't leave this gift under your tree this Christmas Day. Open it and receive everlasting life.

This is how Jesus the Messiah was born. His mother, Mary, was engaged to be married to Joseph. But before the marriage took place, while she was still a virgin, she became pregnant through the power of the Holy Spirit. Joseph, her fiancé, was a good man and did not want to disgrace her publicly, so he decided to break the engagement quietly. As he considered this, an angel of the Lord appeared to him in a dream. "Joseph, son of David," the angel said, "do not be afraid to take Mary as your wife. For the child within her was conceived by the Holy Spirit. And she will have a son, and you are to name him Jesus, for he will save his people from their sins" (Matthew 1:18–21).

CHRISTMASTIME

Christmastime is a time of year
When folks get ready, both far and near,
For the birthday of the Holy One,
The Christ Child, God's only Son.
They sing some songs and get a tree.
They put up lights that they can see.
They spend money and buy many things.
They go to parties. What joy it brings!
They rush around and try to do
All those things that good folks do.
Some give to the poor
and those who are sick.
Some visit the shut-ins
and do it real quick.
They go to church, and when they pray,
They thank the Lord for this special day.
But when that day comes,
as it always will,
They forget the Babe,
and that night so still.

They wake up ready to open their gifts.
They look forward to the way it lifts
Their spirits when that special toy
Is opened by a girl or boy.
They eat and laugh and try to see
All their family members
wherever they may be.
It takes all day to get this done
From the morning time to the setting sun.
When it's time to go to bed that night,
They feel pretty good if all went right.

Did I get the things that I asked for?
Was my family pleased or
did they want more?
Was the cooking all right?
Did the clothes fit them?
Will we do it this way next year again?
They fall asleep so tired and drained.
Ready to rest their bodies and brains.
No one had mentioned the Holy One,
The Christ Child, God's only Son.

This special day at the end of December
The people left out whom they should remember.
What good is all the other things
If the birthday Child is lost in their dreams?
We need to put the Christ Child first.
We need to hunger. We need to thirst
For the gift that comes from up above,
The gift of God's most precious love
For all us sinners who should repent.
This is the reason the Child was sent.

So let's revisit our Christmas Day
And start it right, O Lord, we pray.
Let's give to Jesus first of all.
Let's go to church, not to the mall.
Give Him some time of your busy day.
Stop what you're doing so you can pray.
Give Him your heart. Give Him your soul.
Give Him your life, not a thing withhold.
Read from the Word and take it in.
Apply it to life and grow within.
Help out others. Give to the poor.
Be friends with the friendless. Look for a cure.
Seek to be reconciled to God and to man.
Give peace a chance. Heal the land.

Jesus comes first each day of the year.
Let us worship and praise him
and be of good cheer.
But especially on the day He was born
Let us put Him above all else on that morn.
Begin with Jesus on Christmas Day.
Let Him shine His light to show us the way.
Because only when we seek His face
Can we put Christmas in its proper place.
Not toys. Not gifts. Not little ones.
Not shopping. Not eating. Not being on the run.
Not parties. Not trees. Or any of these things.
Christmas is about Jesus
    and the gift that He brings.

THE TREE

A tree! A tree!
A Christmas tree!
Is this the one
He'd have me see?
The one that's decorated
With bulbs and lights,
The one that we put up
And watch every night,
The one that stands for
The Christmas season,
The one many think
Is the only reason
For our joy,
For our pleasure,
For the happiness
That we treasure,
For our hope,
For our peace,
For our life.

"There's another tree,"
He said to me.
"The one on the hill
At Calvary."
No bulbs. No lights.
No decorations
In the nights.
Does it stand for
A season?
Does it give souls
A reason
For our joy,
For our pleasure,

For the happiness
We treasure,
For our hope,
For our peace,
For our life?

Which one do you see
When you think of Me?
Do you see the beginning
Or do you see the end?
Do you see a child
Or do you see a man?
Do you see the beauty
Or do you see the pain?
Can you experience them both
Or is it not plain
That there's beauty and pain
In both of them?
He was born to die and forgive all our sin.

Both trees are life.
Both trees are death.
Both trees bring freedom.
Both trees bring rest.
Take off the bulbs.
Take off the lights.
Take off the decorations
That we watch every night.
And what you will see
Is a creation of God,
Formed by His hands,
Planted in His sod.
A joy to look at. A beauty to behold
Without all those lights, without being sold.
Just pure and natural as it was meant to be.
Created by Him, a Christmas tree.

Once only a seed
Beginning to grow.
Now a living being
That can truly show
The work of His hand,
The passage of time
The nurturing and growing,
A creation sublime.

Jesus is the tree
Planted by God.
How does the tree look
Planted in your sod?
With bulbs and lights
That are festive and gay,
Or on a hill faraway
In the darkness of day?

Your tree can be both
If the light comes from Him,
Knowing He was born
To die for our sin.

CHRISTMAS COMES

Christmas comes and goes
Each year in late December.
When the season's over
What is it we remember?
The light from the candles
That we can see
The light from the manger
That saved you and me
The gifts that we give
And those we receive
The gift of baby Jesus
For all who believe
The food that we cook
And share with family
The meals that we fix
For the poor community

The songs that we sing
Bringing joy to the air
The hymns that we live
Bringing hope to despair
The people that we visit
The sick and those in jail
Christmas cards, we send
His message in the mail
All the many children
In their holy Christmas plays
Mary, Joseph, shepherds,
And Jesus in the hay.
As Christmas Day is ending
Remember it's *His birth*
The light, the hope, the joy
For everyone on earth.

A Christmas Story

My Savior spoke to me today.
I don't think I heard His call.
It wasn't that I could not hear.
I was shopping at the mall.
It had gotten close to Christmas,
and I had some things to buy.
I had almost finished with my list.
The time was beginning to fly.

I saw those people near the street.
Some were standing by the door.
They were seeking donations for the poor.
I rushed by to enter the store.
Inside the mall were many folks
all busy and hurried too.
The shopping days were dwindling.
Now we only had a few.

An older man was in the store.
He couldn't find the book
That he wanted for his grandchild.
Should I help him out and look?
I thought a moment then did not.
It was getting kind of late.
I had seven presents on my list
and a party to attend at eight.
I bought my book and turned to see
if the man had bought his too.
He was in the back still looking.
Not much that I could do.

I went to get a bite to eat
And found a place to sit.
Right beside me was a rowdy group.
They didn't quite seem to fit.
There were so many of them,
and they made a lot of noise,
A mother and her family,
Three girls and two little boys.
They fussed and fought and made a mess.
It was causing quite a scene.
The mother could not contain herself,
and she seemed to be so mean.

I thought that maybe I could help.
But no, I don't think so.
I don't know those noisy people,
and I really had to go.
The baby was screaming loudly,
and the little girls looked sad.
The boys were running round and round.
I wondered, Where was their dad?

I left this place and pondered,
Could I have helped them out?
I went back to my shopping.
Is this what it's all about?
Spending money here and there.
Buying lots of toys.
Going to parties, eating a lot.
Are these our Christmas joys?
Putting up the Christmas tree
with all the pretty lights
Going to church-related things
and singing "Silent Night."
I went back to my shopping.
Just a few more things to get.
I hoped that I could find them quick,

and that everything would fit.
I rushed back home, got dressed again.
The party was at eight.
If I hurried, I could make it.
I hoped I wouldn't be late.

I went into the church
But found nobody there.
I guess the party was over.
The halls and rooms were bare.
I turned to leave but thought I heard
Someone call my name.
I stopped and listened intently
and heard it once again.
It came from within the church
where all the people sit.
It was kind of dark in there
With only some candles lit.
I sat down in the pews.
The first I had rested that day.
It felt so good to be alone.
I was glad I decided to stay.

I bowed my head and said a prayer
Not thinking of the voice.
But suddenly it was there.
I had to listen. I had no choice.
"My child, I've tried to talk to you
so many times today.
But you were busy shopping.
You couldn't hear what I
had to say.
I put some people in your path
to help you remember me.
But you were in a hurry or maybe
too blind and couldn't see

That there are many people
who just need a helping hand.
You rushed right by each one of them.
There are hundreds in this land.
The people collecting for the poor.
The man looking for the book.
The children when you were eating.
Did you give them a second look?
You came to church tonight
with a party on your mind.
But have you stopped today
to give *Me* a little time?
I left My place in heaven
to come to earth below.
I was born in a stable
and to the cross, I had to go.
I gave My life to save you.
What gift will you give to Me?
Do I have a present in your house?
Is it wrapped up under your tree?"

I sat and stared and realized
That my Lord was speaking to me.
I didn't have a present for Him
Wrapped up and under the tree.
I'd been too busy with other things.
I'd kind of left Him out.
I didn't have time for others.
Isn't this what it's all about?

I stood up very slowly
But before I moved my feet
A tear dropped down from heaven.
I'd made my Savior weep.
I heard His voice once again.
My spirit was lifted anew.
"You're all I want for Christmas."
Then He said, "I love you too."

A Quiet Sacred Moment

It was a quiet, sacred moment
When baby Jesus came to earth.
The Promised One had come.
The prophets told of His birth.
He didn't come in a great display
Of shouts and dazzling lights.
He came in a lowly manger
In the stillness of the night.

Yes, Mary and Joseph knew
He was the Son of God.
The great *I am* from heaven
Looked down and gave a nod
To all the people living here
From faraway and near.
The Savior of the world was born.
He would take away our fear.

Why didn't He come another way?
The people would be glad
If He were born in a palace
And with golden clothes was clad.
With a crown upon His head
And a sword upon His side,
One day, He'd ride a horse
And the nation, He would guide.

Could this little child be the man
To save God's chosen ones,
To rescue all God's family,
His daughters and His sons?

Oh, yes! The angel said,
"I bring good news of joy,
For all the world God sent
His Son, this baby boy."

The angels, the shepherds, the animals,
And Mary and Joseph too
Were present at this holy time.
The Father gave them a view
Of the Messiah, the future King.
He was born in Bethlehem,
Lying in a manger bed.
No room was found at the inn.

He was their Savior, their Promised One.
The people didn't realize
His crown would be of thorns.
A sword would pierce His side.
He wouldn't ride a horse
But a lowly little foal.
Yes, He would lead the nations
By the word the prophets told.

He comes again in silence
In the quiet, still, sweet hour.
He brings God's love and mercy.
He is the holy power
That wipes away our sins,
Who speaks life upon the tomb.
He is the Holy One
Who was born in the Virgin's womb.

Scripture about Christmas

In the sixth month of Elizabeth's pregnancy, God sent the angel Gabriel to Nazareth, a village in Galilee, to a virgin named Mary. "Don't be afraid Mary," the angel told her, "for you have found favor with God! You will conceive and give birth to a son, and you will name him Jesus. He will be very great and will be called the Son of the Most High. The Lord God will give him the throne of his ancestor David. And he will reign over Israel forever; his Kingdom will never end!" Mary asked the angel, "But how can this happen? I am a virgin."

—Luke 1:26, 27a, 30–34

The angel replied, "The Holy Spirit will come upon you, and the power of the Most High will overshadow you. So the baby to be born will be holy, and he will be called the Son of God." Mary responded, "I am the Lord's servant. May everything you have said about me come true."

—Luke 1:35, 38

And because Joseph was a descendant of King David, he had to go to Bethlehem in Judea, David's ancient home. He traveled there from the village of Nazareth in Galilee. He took with him Mary, his fiancée, who was now obviously pregnant. And while they were there, the time came for her baby to be born. She gave birth to her first child, a son. She wrapped him snugly in strips of cloth and laid him in a manger, because there was no lodging available for them.

—Luke 2:4–7

That night there were shepherds staying in the fields, guarding their flocks of sheep. Suddenly an angel of the Lord appeared among them, and the radiance of the Lord's glory surrounded them. They were terribly frightened, but the angel reassured them. "Don't be afraid!" he said. "I bring you good news of great joy for everyone! The Savior—yes, the Messiah, the Lord—has been born tonight in Bethlehem, the city of David!"

—Luke 2:8–11

When the angels had returned to heaven, the shepherds said to each other, "Let's go to Bethlehem! Let's see this thing that has happened, which the Lord has told us about." They hurried to the village and found Mary and Joseph. And there was the baby, lying in the manger.

—Luke 2:15–16

At that time there was a man in Jerusalem named Simeon. He was righteous and devout and was eagerly waiting for the Messiah to come and rescue Israel. The Holy Spirit was upon him and had revealed to him that he would not die until he had seen the Lord's Messiah. That day the Spirit led him to the Temple. So when Mary and Joseph came to present the baby Jesus to the Lord as the Law required, Simeon was there. He took the child in his arms and praising God said, "Sovereign Lord, now let your servant die in peace, as you have promised. I have seen your salvation, which you have prepared for all people. He is a light to reveal God to the nations, and he is the glory of your people Israel."

—Luke 2:25–32

About the Author

Laura Gasque is a former pastor in the UMC and a retired elementary school teacher. She has been writing reflective poetry for her personal faith journey for about thirty years. Her life and work experiences throughout the years and her in-depth study and teaching of the Bible has enabled her to write poetry in a way that allows God to speak to our hearts. Laura loves to absorb the glorious beauty of God's creation by closely observing the sky, the trees and flowers, and the birds and other animals in her surroundings. This is portrayed in some of her poetry. She and her husband, Paul, live in Latta, South Carolina, and look for opportunities to assist and give to others in need. They are the parents of two children, Conan and his wife, Laura, and Lauren and her husband, Davis. They have two fur babies, Peppy and Kitty, who love and entertain them and keep them active.

CPSIA information can be obtained
at www.ICGtesting.com
Printed in the USA
FSHW010902071021
85287FS

9 781636 301662